A Recent Imagining

A RECENT IMAGINING

—— Interviews with ——

HAROLD BLOOM
GEOFFREY HARTMAN
J. HILLIS MILLER
PAUL DE MAN

Robert Moynihan

1986 ———————————————— ARCHON BOOKS

© 1986 Robert Moynihan. All rights reserved.
First published 1986 as an Archon Book,
an imprint of The Shoe String Press, Inc.
Hamden, Connecticut 06514

Printed in the United States of America

The paper in this book meets the guidelines
for permanence and durability
of the Committee on Production Guidelines
for Book Longevity of the Council on Library Resources.

Set in Sabon by Brevis Press, Bethany, Connecticut.
Designed by Jill Breitbarth.

Library of Congress Cataloging-in-Publication Data

A Recent imagining.
    1. Critics—United States—Interviews.   I. Bloom,
Harold.   II. Moynihan, Robert, 1936–   .
PN74.R43   1986   801'.95'0973   86–17445
ISBN 0–208–02120–5 (alk. paper)

The interview with Paul de Man appeared in *The Yale Review,* Volume LXXIII,
Summer, 1984, and portions of the interviews with Geoffrey Hartman and with
Harold Bloom were in *boundary* 2, Volume IX, Fall, 1980, and in *Diacritics,* Volume
XIII, Fall, 1983. Part of the interview with J. Hillis Miller appeared in *Criticism,*
Volume XXIV, no. 2, 1982.

Photographs of Harold Bloom, Geoffrey Hartman, J. Hillis Miller, and Paul de Man
are by T. Charles Erickson, Yale University Office of Public Information. Reprinted
by permission.

For Moira and Brigit

A recent imagining of reality,

Much like a new resemblance of the sun,
Down-pouring, up-springing and inevitable,
A larger poem for a larger audience . . .

> *from*
> "An Ordinary Evening in New Haven"
> *by Wallace Stevens*

CONTENTS

INTRODUCTION

One of the first year copies of Jacques Derrida's *Glas* posed a threat to the neatness and tidiness usually associated with literary comment in most of its forms. Why, a Yale librarian wrote the Paris publisher in the mid-1970s, were the first pages of the book omitted? Would the publisher please remedy this error and provide a complete copy of the book? The note in French must be every European's dream of response to the upstart Yankee. In fact, the Galilée Press-person answered, the text does begin without the first pages. A photocopy of this note on the publisher's letterhead is now neatly affixed to the title page of the book in the Yale Library. Yet the question remains: How is it possible to have a book begin on page seven? Where's the rest of it?

These interviews do not claim to provide the rest of it, but the motivation for this work did arise, at least in part, to make Bloom, Hartman, Miller, and de Man, three of whom somewhat mirror the deconstructionist lamp, more extemporaneously accessible to a wider reading public. Not every critical response, fair and unfair to this group, could be answered in writing, yet authors always want to respond to reviewers and commentators. In addition, from listening to two of the subjects of this book read and lecture during National Endowment for the Humanities seminars and on less and more formal occasions, I recognized a difference between their writing and verbal expression. So the rhetorical with its directness and clarity seemed worth preserving.

As for the historical precedent for such an enterprise? A not totally friendly English acquaintance was kind enough to sketch a historical background of the interview. It was, he said, both typically American in the worship of celebrity and an expression of the worst aspects of eighteenth and nineteenth century sycophancy towards the cultural "figgers" (or "figgahs"). The historical models, he said, range from the earliest examples in continental literature, the pious doubters seeking answers at Delphi, to the credulous tourists questioning Goethe and Emerson, and our own contemporary journalists seeking truth but recording only deceptions.

But to change the referents of my acquaintance, I did not make the trips to New Haven with even that small amount of veneration that the *Paris Review* questioners adopt toward their "creative" subjects, the *Playboy* interviewers towards their culturally dappled victims, or even, in the good old days of the 1940s, 50s and early 60s, the acerbic questions of Lawrence Spivak on "Meet the Press." Certainly the veneration of the pilgrim visiting the ex-sage Emerson or Goethe did not inform any particle of this enterprise.

Nor, in a different way of approaching these interviews, do the questions validate their subjects (they're already "valid"). They merely address questions of logic and appropriateness. At times, ignorance in the questions is feigned, at other times not. Most efforts to control the direction and matter of the answers, no matter what the preparation, was a failure. So the Socratic method, if it were a precedent with its many demotic offshoots, is also not a model. Socrates seemed to *know* the answers.

Nonetheless, anyone who has ever conducted an interview knows that the occasion and its record are in large part the illusion of the impromptu. An adequate interviewer will have read extensively about her or his subjects and will have discovered their biases. There is also the question of accuracy in an interview. Is what is said either excised or edited for the benefit of the subject? Also, what is the relation of the interviewer to the subject? Were the two eating dinner, sipping wine, smoking cigars? Or in H. L. Mencken's paraphrase, who bought the tickets for the concert's reviewer?

The answers to these reasonable doubts are simple. First, nobody bought the tickets—there was no grant money. Every subject that found its way to a question and answer remains. I interrupted the speakers when there seemed to be some tentative or real contradiction or when a response appeared to need clarification. Finally, the interviews were serious, not social occasions.

Of course, no preparation readies an interviewer for the surprise of some of the responses. In order and without preference, Harold Bloom's description of his meeting with Wallace Stevens, his wicked comments about Adrienne Rich and other "poets," his reservations about the academic enterprise of Jewish Studies, his lambasting of Hilton Kramer—his polemical gifts in general—always surprise.

Geoffrey Hartman's comments which follow are antithetical, and not merely for their modulated and skillfully balanced casuistry. Hartman disagrees with Bloom about the nature of Jewish Studies and its newly found place in the secular American curriculum. He also comments more directly on Derrida than the others, helping fill in those "lost" pages, those missing days of formulaic creation. Hartman also surprises with his comments on some of the political and historical issues arising from the Reagan-Bitburg fiasco. Hillis Miller's remarks about his upstate New York childhood were also a surprise, and his story about Harold Bloom's first sighting of a cow in Ithaca's rural suburbs is an anecdotal and comedic high point of this enterprise. As with nearly everyone who heard him, I too was delighted with Paul de Man's exactitude in oral statement. His comment on texts and irony is worthy of any writer in the history of European skepticism: "There is no valid text, but some invalid texts are more validly invalid than others!" De Man's interview was taken at our first meeting, in a single session in 1980, and appears here as printed posthumously in *The Yale Review* in 1984.

The other interviews were done at different times between 1979 and 1985, and the earlier sessions appeared in *Diacritics, boundary 2,* and *Criticism.* I thank those journals for allowing the republication of the earlier and partial transcripts. This project was the first extensive group of interviews with this body of "mere critics," and began without the recent books by Daniel O'Hara, Douglas Atkins, Frank Lentricchia, Grant Webster, and the seemingly centrifugal efforts of many others. Anyone wishing to find the unabating negative critical reactions to the "Yale Critics" may encounter them in different issues of *The Hudson Review, The London Review of Books, The Harvard Alumni Bulletin* (!), *The American Scholar, The New Criterion,* and different corn and barley ricks, some of which are here sampled in the questions and their responses.

Always there is a tendency for the witnesses of academic debates, even if they are fellow academicians, to define the issues as unimportant, merely verbal. Perversely, several academic careers have been scuttled because of opposition to the ideas expressed in these critical controversies. Colin MacCabe was denied tenure for practicing some of the new arts in part discussed here, and a full transcript of a meeting of the Cambridge Senate is extant in *The Cambridge University Reporter,* February 18, 1981. One of the basic issues of this university discussion appears to be that the discipline of literature and language "professing" is a nomistic calling; that is, it is a species of divine revelation, self-defined and absolute. All of the British dons in this discussion believe that the teaching of literature is a serious calling (so serious that it could perhaps best be entrusted to the less divinely inspired). Yet, while the tones and syntax are British (the participants actually speak in balanced sentences and complete paragraphs), there is not a whit of essential difference between the English don and Our American Cousin, the U.S. professor. It is fairly obvious, given invisibility and anonymity, that some professors would kill for their prejudices. Failing that, they will combine in committee meetings and on editorial boards to reject the dangerous and the heretic in all their forms, verbal and personified. Discussing the sacking of would-be-don MacCabe, for instance, Mr. H. Sykes Davies says of a former unpleasantness about "personnel matters":

> My telephone rang one evening, and when I answered it someone asked if I was the Chairman of the Faculty . . . and wished to be told if it was true that Mr so-and-so had been denied his undue promotion again. I slightly disguised my voice and said that I would be glad to have the second fitting of that suit whenever he liked—that I would get my diary, and so on. Whatever he asked, I held firmly to my view that it was a call from some tailor about my suit.

Like many American cousins, this don distrusts the foreign, that across-the-Atlantic or Dover other:

> One strange rogue element that has somehow wandered into these discussions is something called structuralism. Like all other Parisian fashions it is very passing. And like all words that end in the suffix *-ism* it has no ascertained meaning—always excepting "prism," and perhaps "schism."

Mr. H. H. Erskine-Hill lowers his comments to a moral condemnation of recent trends, echoing the xenophobic rhetoric of the Cold War:

> What has emerged as the most decadent and absurd strain in structuralism is . . . aptly called "cognitive atheism": the view that one interpretation is as valid as another. . . . [S]oft Marxism

is interested, one may suspect, because it seems to permit of a broad mythologizing of cultural phenomena, invulnerable to the possible recalcitrance or denial of evidence.

One of the Yale group talks and writes a good deal about "precursors." The precedent texts for these comments are *Butley*, "Shooting an Elephant," and a speech U.S. Senator Homer Capehart delivered attacking immorality in the 1940s.

While I am no partisan of the four interviewed here, their mental acuity and power of expression far transcend the abilities of most of their antagonists, who for the most part repeat the most tiresome of forensic tactics. There was a time, an imaginary and quite distant Golden Age, when the strategies of *ad hominem, non sequitur,* and oversimplified analogy were to be found mainly in political diatribe. These dubious arts have now passed into the formerly sacred and virginal groves of academic literary comment. Their success may in part be a "sign of the age,"—except, of course, that such cliches are the most absurd kind of critical fiction. French or French derived comments on art, politics, or anything else have always been detested in England, and conformity of the most absurd degree has always been practiced in the U.S., as a famous French visitor, a very high-toned skeptic, remarked some 150 years ago. As for the dogmas of a moral aesthetic, the critically minded may remember that the most absurd comments about humanity and art are usually made under the influence of creeds and publicly decanted religion. Dogma always in some ways kills its incessant repeaters, quite before their official departures to the nether.

My own favorite skeptic, however, was the English don Henry Sidgwick, the great debunker of Kant. Sidgwick once attended such meetings as those at Cambridge almost just quoted. Perhaps he strides more comfortably, however, as an antecedent to these proceedings of question and answer. Therefore his quite rigorous objections to Matthew Arnold shall begin these pages. Sidgwick was most concerned with a kind of form and function, the logical coherence of statements and the perceivable results of theoretical discussions. To answer my British acquaintance, these words and others of Sidgwick informed my part in this enterprise:

It is because he ignores this antagonism [between religion and culture], which seems to me so clear and undeniable if stated without the needless and perilous exaggerations which preachers have used about it, that I have called Mr. Arnold perverse. A philosopher [Hegel] with whom he is more familiar than I am speaks, I think, of "the reconciliation of antagonisms" as the essential feature of the most important steps in the progress of humanity. I seem to see profound truth in this conception, and perhaps Mr. Arnold has intended to realize it. But, in order to reconcile antagonisms, it is needful to probe them to the bottom; whereas Mr. Arnold skims over them with a lightly-worn tranquility that irritates instead of soothing.

> —*from* "The Prophet of Culture," a review of
> *Culture and Anarchy* in *Macmillan's
> Magazine,* August 1867

HAROLD BLOOM

Would you like to say something about your early career at Cornell with M. H. Abrams? Were you interested in Abrams because of the Romantic poets, or did he introduce you to them?

I don't think that he introduced me to the study of the Romantics, though he was indeed one of my first teachers at Cornell. I had been intensely interested in Blake from the time that I was twelve or thirteen years old. The first poets who captured me were Hart Crane when I was about eleven, and then Blake when I was twelve or thirteen. I doubt that I had much understanding of what either of them was writing, but I was, because of them, intensely involved in Romantic poetry.

How did you discover them?

Without anyone introducing me to it, when I was nine or ten, I was very interested, just on my own, in reading poetry. I was an inveterate patron of our local branch library there in the Bronx. It was quite a good branch library, and they had a substantial collection of poetry. And I took out—I can't remember which poets at the beginning, probably anthologies—but then I went on quite quickly to Hart Crane, whose language and rhythm fascinated me. I went from Crane to Blake, including the long poems which I read entirely in terms of their rhetorical urgency.

Did you read these aloud at the beginning or were you able to imagine the sound from the print without reciting?

Oh no, no. I chanted them to myself. I also discovered when very young, even before then, and no doubt it is hereditary and has to do with ancestors who were Talmudists, that I had an astonishing memory, particularly for verbatim recall of poetry. A number of the poems by Crane, by Blake, and others that I first learned to recite out loud to myself by the time I was thirteen, I still retain verbatim today.

Crane's poem "To Brooklyn Bridge"—does that stand out prominently in your memory for its sound and sense of the city?

No, I don't think Crane's poem had that much to do with my sense of the city. It was the invocatory strain, the kind of high sense of Pindaric invocation summoning the poetic powers, the sense of glory. I don't think it had much to do with any referential aspect as such.

What is so unusual about this description is the difference between the appeal of the sound of poetry, the higher orders of sound, and the usual manner in which poetry exists in teaching and criticism, most of which assumes that poetry is not a sensory, or sensual experience, but has much more to do with the order of print.

Well, I assume in the criticism that I write, and I would assume that most critics believe this, that there is a basis upon which the teacher builds the elements which you mentioned. I suppose, fundamentally, that they precede teaching, the kind of teaching that one is called upon to do with advanced undergraduates or graduate students.

Are there aspects of the Jewish religious services, of song, that reinforce this approach to the sound of literature?

There is clearly the invocatory strain in Biblical poetry, in the Song of Deborah, from the Book of Judges and the Song of Moses, and in the Psalms, and of course in Isaiah, and Jeremiah. Of course, Crane and Blake both have a song-like quality, and they are both, though in very different ways, religious, incantatory poets. What I did acquire from Mike Abrams, early on, was what was already strongly present in his teaching back around 1948 when I was first his student, which eventually became the pattern of displacement of religious models that he studied in his book *Natural Supernaturalism*.

One of the obvious things about your criticism is the generous amount of quotation you give your subjects. That is, there's often enough quotation to sense the voice of the writer. Is your early discovery of the voice within print the reason for such quotation?

There is an intense relationship between the totality of the body and the totality of sensory apprehension and poetry. But I've never tried to deal with that overtly in my criticism. It's the kind of thing that John Hollander does better than anyone else in his book *Vision and Resonance*.

But both the visual and the auditory aspect of poems for me mark an earlier phase of both my experience of poetry and also what I take to be the concern of critical activity.

Let me refer again to the manner in which literature is discussed. It might strike many people reading criticism that everything is dealt with except the language of poetry. In other words, the critic talks about forms, about symbols, but where is the language itself?

There is the difficulty that so much of the full effect of the language lies outside the area of cognitive apprehension, and since the study of poetry is essentially cognitive, since it has got to be rational before it can be more than rational—I guess, with the exception of Hollander, I just don't know of any criticism that has been able to deal with these aspects of poetry.

There is nothing more tiresome than the sort of thing that Edith Sitwell used to do when she would explain that the effect of the splendor of some particular word was because of all the *k*'s at this point or the *l*'s at that point. Clearly, this doesn't do anybody any good at all. It's purely affective. It's almost the sort of matter that criticism has got to convey between its lines.

There are elaborate methods of sound and rhetorical patterns in the Renaissance, the English Renaissance, imitations of the "figures of Gorgias" found in John Lyly. But there is a great leap between those patterns and Shakespeare, or even Wyatt and Surrey, that might be inexplicable except in the sounding of the language itself. Would you like to make a comment on that?

No.

Does T. S. Eliot strike you as an invocatory, verbal presence?

Yes, oh yes. I would think that the larger aspects of his abiding power are most certainly in his voice, that he is the continuer of both Tennyson and Whitman in that respect. There is that elegiac intensity, that ominously haunting sense that you get of the music of poetry in him which accounts for his continued popularity, by now even with relatively ordinary readers.

So that The Waste Land *is . . .*

A collection of magnificent fragments, highly Tennysonian, highly Whitmanian, with much of the same sort of lyrical power that both of those poets have.

How do you regard Eliot's statement about the impersonalized, even depersonalized, role of the poet given in "Tradition and the Individual Talent"?

I regard it as a mere subterfuge or evasion on his part. I don't find it of any real cognitive interest. It's a self-serving defense.

Do you think it was a strategy because he was aware of the academic and analytic approach to verse?

No. I don't think that's where the major cause of it would lie. He waged a polemic, as we all know, an extreme polemic, although he was extraordinarily successful with a literary public in making his polemic look like literary history itself, whatever one takes that

The art or practice of controversy or disputation —

to be. He had a polemic against his actual precursors that would include, primarily, Tennyson and Whitman, or even Pater, as a British instance, or even, as he stands behind all American poetry, Emerson. Eliot, therefore, in a rather familiar pattern of poetic evasion, insisted on seventeenth-century forebears, insisted upon Dante, insisted upon nineteenth-century French forebears so as to put both himself and his reader off the track.

But it seems clearer and clearer that a poem like *Maud* or a poem like *In Memoriam,* or perhaps more than any poem ever written, Whitman's "When Lilacs Last in the Dooryard Bloomed," are the real precursor texts for Eliot's poetry.

There are conventional ways of viewing what you have called "precursor texts" in conventional literary history, the contrast and comparison of older works and their later influences, such as Italian literature and its influence on English sixteenth-century literature, the relations between Greek and Roman literature, Keats returning to an imitated Spenserian diction, the whole matter of literal "influences" such as Livingston Lowes' treatment of Coleridge's "Rime of the Ancient Mariner." By "predecessor," however, you mean something much different that is partly explained in your Anxiety of Influence. What is the difference between the older approach of "influence" and what you have called "predecessor"? In other words, Eliot leaps across the constraints of time to avoid recognizing his more immediate forebears?

I think most instances of authentic poetic influence take place very directly between older contemporaries and younger contemporaries, or between generations, whether actual generations or literary ones. Eliot's poetry is very deeply—in its actual staple, its range of sensibility, its question of the poet's relation to his own poetry, in terms of rhetorical stance, the relation between poetry and history—Eliot's poetry deeply and essentially rebels against inadequate followers of Tennyson: Edwardian and to some extent Georgian poetry, and also what you could call the American Pre-Raphaelitism which succeeded the great age of Whitman. Nevertheless, what Eliot went back to is not what his criticism asserted he was going back to.

In a very deep sense he goes back to a composite precursor,

whose major elements are Tennyson and Whitman, just as in Pound the major elements in the precursor are Browning and Whitman, and in William Carlos Williams the composite precursor is formed of Keats and Whitman.

If you look at Williams's earliest poetry you find that his dominant figures, his idea of a poem and his idea of a poet come from his reading of Keats's poetry. I find it both fascinating and inevitable that in his last phase in a poem like "Asphodel, That Greeny Flower," he is essentially, in a transumptive way, returning to the Keats of the odes and of the *Hyperions*.

Are the influences and relations between these poets verbal as well as intellectual?

There is obviously the whole problem of allusion and echo which is very difficult and on which I would cite *The Figure of Echo* by Hollander, because I think he is better on these aspects of poetry than any other critic, or in this case, poet-critic.

There is the question of direct and indirect allusion and echo, the question of repressed allusion and echo, but no, I would look at what I believe to be more fundamental aspects of poetry. I think we know very little as yet about the actual processes by which one active reading produces another active reading, which would include one small category within that larger one, of the way in which one poem helps to form another. There are many, many different levels of depth or the reader's apprehension in which these processes are manifest.

There are all the visible elements, and they would include those aspects which usually are said to be ascertainable and evidentiary in interpoetic relationships. But then there is much more complex material because one has to begin to study a poem in terms of what is not there, even though it should be, or might be, or could be, or almost *is* there.

Now this, of course, makes positivistic critics and scholars very nervous, but I think this is a much more interesting and vital area in which interpoetic relationships tend to cluster. That is, what is it which is missing or all but present in a poem, what is suggested or evaded? That is usually, I think, a much better path, or hidden path, hidden channel, for what is taking place between two poems. I am aware that it is extremely difficult to demonstrate such evidence for these relationships, but perhaps *evidence* is a very bad term for it in any case. Yet, the shape or form, in any sense of form a poem assumes, has a great deal to do with hidden pressures upon it. To a considerable extent, I try to study those hidden pressures.

You wrote your first book while a graduate student at Yale. Would you like to say something about that work on Shelley?

It was a dissertation supervised by Frederick Pottle. It was written, mostly, in 1954 and 1955, and was later revised, largely, by 1957. It was published January 1959. I haven't looked at it for a great many years, and I suspect that much of it would make me uncomfortable. There was a lot of idealizing in it about the nature of poetry and the nature of interpoetic relationships.

You prominently mention Buber in the introduction.

Yes. My attitude toward Buber has changed a great deal through the years. As late as the time that I was finishing the work on Yeats back around '68 to '69, when I wrote the last of six or seven versions of that book, I was still deeply uncomfortable with Gnosticism, whether in Yeats or in myself or in anyone else, and I still tended to subscribe to Buber's view on the matter, but I'd already grown very uneasy with Buber, especially under the influence of reading Gershom Scholem. In these ten years and more I suppose Scholem has in every way replaced Buber for me. I now find Buber quite unreadable, a hopeless idealizer and someone who refused to see his own Gnosticism or the deep Gnosticism that is the actual basis of the Hasidic movement, as Scholem has demonstrated so overwhelmingly. I tried to handle this issue of confronting Gnosticism particularly in the chapter on Yeats in the book *Poetry and Repression*.

Could you explain what you mean by the term "idealizing"?

The reading of poetry, the writing of poetry, the nature of poetry, the nature of the poet have all been consistently overidealized throughout the last hundred and fifty or even two hundred years. This goes on continuously in the whole cultural enterprise of English departments and the study of literature in general in this country and in Britain.

Do you mean the kind of idealism or descendant of idealism that the Cambridge Platonists philosophically and culturally instituted in the seventeenth century?

No, I mean idealized in the Arnoldian sense. Quite specifically, I think Arnold is the major culprit and precursor of this modern mode of idealizing in his view that poetry was spilt religion, in his view that as religion died the future of poetry would be immense because its cultural, educational and spiritual value would be enhanced. I think it is this view which Arnold communicated so successfully to the academies and indeed to the whole critical enterprise in our time, so that on a popular level, in Britain and America in particular, it is the supposed justification for the serious study of poetry and literature, and in many people, for the critical enterprise as such.

Of course, it has produced this curious phenomenon of what one could only call the Clerisy, the sense in which the academic legions in the study of literature have become the kind of Protestant pastors or secular rabbis or defrocked priests of a curious kind of secular religion. So I mean "idealizing" in that sense, and I was a terrible offender in this regard. My ideas began to change fundamentally when I wrote a version of what eventually became the first chapter of *The Anxiety of Influence*. I think that I wrote that in the summer of 1967 or so.

Was that your English Institute paper on Coleridge from approximately the same period?

That isn't what I am referring to. In the summer of 1967 I wrote a long sort of prose rhapsody called "The Covering Cherub of Poetic Influence." Eventually six years later in greatly cut down, revised, and to some extent historicized guise, it became the first chapter of *The Anxiety of Influence,* the chapter called "Clinamen."

One of the things that might strike a reader of Arnold is that while he presents what you have called an "idealization," he limits the vocabulary of discovery. There is no reason to cite again for negative examination his use of the "touchstone" or examples of what he considered the greatest abbreviated samples of poetry, but his use of the term real *or* really *several times in one paragraph of* Culture and Anarchy *would make a reader at least vaguely unhappy with both repetition of language and limitation of means. Is criticism of this kind an evasion?*

It's tendentious, in the highest.

Were you ever drawn toward Arnold at all at any time?

No. I always found him a flat and flawed poet.

Has he an ear for the sound of poetic language?

He has no ear, either inner or outer. The poetry with but two or three exceptions is anything but distinguished. I regard him, as I have remarked in *The Anxiety of Influence* and I guess elsewhere, as one of the prime sufferers from that aspect of the anxiety of influence that produces weak poets, and Arnold, I believe, is very much one of the exemplars of the weak poet. He had nothing good at any time through all his criticism of his correspondence to say about the poetry of Keats. One would not think that Keats would have mattered to him at all. It should be much more of a scandal to readers than it is to read side by side the major odes of Keats and then to read "Thyrsis" and "The Scholar Gypsy," because again and again the stances of the Arnoldian elegies owe everything to Keats's odes, and either Arnold is unconscious of this or he is simply evasive. I think it is the first. I think that it is so deeply repressed that he is incapable of confronting this difficulty and that we have the embarrassment of absolute and involuntary echoing of Keats all through those two poems by Arnold.

Do you think the snobbery of the English class system was an impediment for Arnold?

Oh, I dare say that it was, but I'm not much given to social analysis of literary matters.

Why, if Arnold is so weak or at least a poet that has to be so qualified, has he passed so insistently into anthologies?

Well, he was of course a great "anthologizer" himself; he is the deviser of touchstones, a canonizer. Someone who is a great

canonizer and great finder and exponent of touchstones is clearly
going to be highly available to those who come after him who can-
onize or who would make touchstones. He was, for awhile, a professor of poetry, and he's surely the ancestor and precursor of most
modern professors of poetry. He is the poet of professors, as Eliot
and then Auden became the poets of professors in our time. Arnold
is a poet with whom people with an academic sensibility are very
much at home.

I don't think Arnold should have this position with academicians. I find Ruskin and Pater and Wilde, who are a tradition, much
more effective and powerful critics of literature, poetry, and of criticism itself than Arnold is. Arnold's sensibility seems to me very
crude compared to that of Ruskin, Pater, or Oscar Wilde. It's quite
clearly the tradition that moves from Ruskin through Pater and
Wilde that interests me and which I would certainly want to set up
more as a model for the professorial or academic criticism of poetry
than the Arnoldian, Eliotic line.

*Do you think that Americans so emphasize ideas of utility and im-
provement, supposedly evidentiary proof of the social good or result
of most of what they do, that Arnold is adopted as a partial model
of social relevance?*

There is certainly a kind of Arnoldian element that helped to
produce Lionel Trilling and which Trilling himself celebrated in
Arnold.

What kind of training would present Arnold to Trilling as a model?

In the early thirties the social concern was so great that the
notion was that poetry and all literature and criticism had to be
socially engaged. And there is Arnold, who does indeed worry at
length about the relationship between poetry and society.

Isn't Freud more important to Trilling, however, than was Arnold?

It's as fair, probably, to characterize Trilling as a Freudian critic
as an Arnoldian one. I would say that what saved Trilling as a critic
was Freud, saved him from some of the worst consequences of Ar-
noldianism, and made Trilling as critic *qua* critic more interesting
than Eliot was.

Wasn't Marx also influential on Trilling's book about Arnold?

I'm so much of a different tradition that I don't really have much to say about Arnold or even Trilling, whom I liked very much personally and was associated with in editing the *Oxford Anthology.* His best essays are certainly remarkable, but I don't feel that I have much that would be useful or interesting to say on Arnoldian criticism. It's just not my kind.

How was this greeted when you arrived at Yale? The syllabus for the introductory course in literature had been prepared by several, including Cleanth Brooks.

It was very much under his influence and that of Robert Penn Warren, and I believe that Professors Mack and Martz and others, who were very much in the tradition of Brooks and Warren, and W. K. Wimsatt, who had something to do with drawing up the curriculum. It represented a consensus of the senior people in the department. I don't think it differed greatly here from a great many other places, though this was probably one of the leading institutions in bringing about that kind of change. The standard line of poets as you were supposed to teach them was the quite justified one of Chaucer (these are non-dramatic, of course)—Chaucer, Spenser, Donne, Milton, Pope, Wordsworth, and then quite suddenly at the end, Eliot. I tended at first to substitute Tennyson, and then increasingly I substituted Stevens for Eliot. I notice that I was a sort of precursor, even though I never tried to be an influence in this regard, because I gather that this is what many of the younger people teaching here now do. There has been a kind of general displacement of Eliot by Stevens.

Did you have any contact with Stevens while he was still alive?

Yes, just once. What year would that have been? Was it in 1949 that he read the short version of "An Ordinary Evening in New Haven" at The Connecticut Academy of Arts and Sciences? I was in New York, down from Cornell at the time, where I was an undergraduate. Being already greatly fascinated with his poetry from about 1947 on, I heard that he was going to be reading a new, long poem. I came up and attended the reading, uninvited, and was as greatly puzzled by "An Ordinary Evening in New Haven" in the shorter version as anybody in the audience was. He did not read it very well on that occasion. He droned.

But then afterwards, I, again uninvited, attended the reception. He was so formidable a figure that he was standing by himself. At one point I had the courage to approach him and we had a brief conversation, which I inaugurated, about Shelley, in the course of which I asked him his general judgment of Shelley as a poet. He said that he was ambivalent. It was probably not the word he used. He suggested both reservations and intense admiration and then moved and astonished me by quoting aloud a stanza of "The Witch of Atlas" which he had by heart, the stanza beginning, "Men scarcely know how beautiful fire is. . . ."

I realized since how permeated with Shelley his poetry is, much more so even than I indicated in my book on Stevens; in particular, I would say now, with Shelley's prose *Defense of Poetry.*

I remember talking about that in the book, but I didn't realize how extensive it was. There are certain passages in "Notes toward a Supreme Fiction" that I had not realized even then, which I realize now, are echoes, whether suppressed or deliberately repressed or deliberate, of *A Defense of Poetry.*

Of course, I now see him as being, like Shelley, essentially a Lucretian poet and therefore very much in Shelley's tradition.

In what sense do you mean Lucretian?

In his visionary skepticism, in his ultimate metaphysics, in his attitude towards what once would have been called the gods, in his attitude towards nature, in his general view of human nature and destiny.

We know how complex Lucretius is. There is a strong Lucretian element in Shelley and Whitman, just as there is, of course, an overtly Lucretian element in Stevens, just as there is an overtly Epicurean and Lucretian element in the ideology and sensibility of Walter Pater.

Tennyson has a well-known attack on Lucretius.

Tennyson has a deeply uneasy and very powerful poem "Lucretius," but the attack would evidence how much Lucretian sensibility he feared to find in himself.

Whereas Shelley would have celebrated it?

Shelley is clearly celebrating Lucretius in a number of passages in *Prometheus Unbound* and elsewhere. But that kind of, it could only be an oxymoron, that kind of visionary materialism that one finds in Lucretius, in Shelley, in Whitman, in Pater, is clearly a major element in Stevens.

You have not only the book on Stevens but several essays. Are you writing more about him?

Now I think I'm rather burned out on Stevens. I can still teach it with real intensity. But even though there are things that I would still like to say, I doubt that I will write about Stevens again.

You once mentioned that you read Stevens every day for a good many years.

For many, many years I read Stevens. From 1947 until the mid-1970s I tended to read Stevens all but daily. He was the poet I found most congenial. He probably pervades all of my language and all of my procedures.

I once asked this before but would like to repeat the question. Is it possible that you have read him so consistently that your theory of poetry and poetic forebears comes from that reading? Did you not use Stevens as a positive but inverse example of his own use of the past, and isn't Stevens's use of the literary past partly incorporated in your own theories of poetic creation?

I'm still not sure that I can handle the question. To a considerable extent, the way in which I read all of the Romantic poets, all of the nineteenth-century poets, the way I read Whitman is all powerfully conditioned by my reading of Stevens and by what I would say is Stevens's implicit reading of romantic tradition, of Whitman in particular.

I think that's what I asked four or five years ago, if you had not moved from Stevens to the interpretation of the past.

Yes, I think that's true. I think I've tended to use Stevens as a kind of point of arrival and departure. That is to say, I tended to read poets before Stevens, at least post-Wordsworthian poets and post-Emersonian poets in America in ways which are strongly altered by my reading of Stevens, and I certainly more explicitly have tended to read American poetry since Stevens very much in his light.

I would like to ask another question about a somewhat biographical matter concerning your critical productivity before the Stevens book appeared. It was . . .

Intense. It has not been so intense since I finished the Stevens book in 1976. It was published a year later in 1977. From 1976 until now I have written relatively little criticism. There are three or four published essays and three or four that have not yet been published and some notebook material. I have fallen off, except that during a year and a half over that time I wrote a visionary novel, a speculative fiction, *A Flight to Lucifer,* but for various personal reasons I was writing very intensely from about 1973 to about 1976.

There were three works of criticism, or four, immediately before the Stevens study?

I would have to count. After *The Anxiety of Influence* came *A Map of Misreading* in 1975, *Kabbalah and Criticism* in 1975, *Poetry and Repression,* and *Figures of Capable Imagination,* both of them in 1976, and then the Stevens book in 1977. So I guess that is six books counting *The Anxiety of Influence.*

One of the two things that most seems to affect your critics is the addition of vocabulary that you defined in The Anxiety of Influence. . .

Yes, which I have kept using and modifying ever since.

The second is, of course, your productivity during that period. You seemed to mystify academicians by the sheer amount of your work during this time. What took you on this productive flight, which is remarkable whether or not one agrees or disagrees with your method and terminology? How did you physically do that much writing? Where did you find the time and energy?

I wasn't sleeping much during that period.

Did you write your manuscripts in longhand?

I can't type. I write it out. Well, I tend to use notebooks. Much less so now in the last three years. But of course, there is a deceptive element in all this. That period was the culmination of many years of work. I had published three early books in '59, '61, and '63, *The Visionary Company* in 1961 and *Blake's Apocalypse* in 1963. I published a commentary in the Erdman volume on Blake in 1965, and all through those years following I wrote the essays that came out in *Ringers in the Tower* in 1971. But from 1967 down to 1973 I was very much at work first on finishing a book on Yeats by 1970 and also on the texts, my own texts, that appeared in *The Anxiety of Influence,* and then from '73 to '76 I drew considerably on note-book material and of course, sustained meditation. The productivity of 1973 to 1976 was the product of a time that had gone on really from 1963, when my book on Blake appeared, down to 1973. So there were ten years of meditation, reading, notetaking, of thinking, behind that burst of three years of composition. As I say, I have not written very much except for this visionary novel in three years now, and at the moment, am disturbed by how difficult it is to write.

But I don't believe that it was the productivity that bothered my many unamiable and negative critics. I don't believe that for a moment.

Was it the introduction of a new critical vocabulary?

No, I don't think it was that either. I don't believe that it has anything to do with vocabulary or with the mode or the manner. I have given some thought to it, and I don't like to talk much about this, because as I say, most of the attacks are mere abuse and not worth my time. But if I were to sum up the negative reactions to my work, I think there are two primary causes: one is that if there is discourse about anxiety it is necessarily going to induce anxiety. It will represent a return of the repressed for a great many people.

The second, and I think this is the much more overt and I think is the main cause, I have been increasingly demonstrating or trying to demonstrate that every possible stance a critic, a scholar, a teacher can take towards a poem is itself inevitably and necessarily po-etic. That it is tropological, that no matter how humble, earnest, devoted, on his knees the critic or scholar or teacher is, that is just as much a fiction as any other stance towards a poem, as say, my stance towards a poem is. This is found intolerable, deeply unsettling by many, many people, whether they are professional journalists or, even more, professional academicians. I think they find that it calls their status and function much more into question than they can bear.

Their willing subservience?

Well, you know, the supposed positivistic basis for their activity is put into question, and their humility is exposed as a self-deception.

The reason I ask this is that there is no one else writing criticism at the present who causes such a pathology of response, or reaction which poses as critical response. Or is the response "critical"?

No, it's not. Frank McConnell, whose review of my novel was in *The New Republic,* said that the response to my critical work on the part of many academicians and journalists was the sort of reaction you would expect either pornography or religious heresy to provoke. I think there is something in that.

You don't think of yourself as a heretic?

What do you mean by heretic?

As cited from McConnell.

Well, he must have meant in some former age when a heretic could provoke that kind of response. There is a Gnostic stance in my work. It has now become wholly explicit. It is, I think, the deepest basis for my work as it is in my novel, which concerns itself with it. But there is no such thing as religious heresy anymore because there is no such thing as religious orthodoxy anymore. What there are, are unchallenged assumptions, unchallenged metaphysical assumptions, unchallenged epistemological assumptions, unchallenged procedural assumptions in every field of academic study, but particularly in the study of literature. It has become clearer and clearer to me that every mode of criticism that I know, or almost every mode, is founded upon metaphysical, epistemological and general philosophical stances to which I give no assent. The whole basis of western criticism tends to be a blend of Aristotelianism and Platonism in different modifications. I am much more interested in ancient modes of criticism that go more to Stoic philosophy or Epicurean philosophy.

Such works as Brooks's and Wimsatt's Literary Criticism: A Short History . . .

Platonism and Aristotelianism, Christian Platonism and Christian Aristotelianism . . .

Some recent schools of criticism use Aristotle, particularly The Poetics, *as their basis.*

I've never found it adequate as a model. I've never found those aspects of the critical tradition to be of great help.

The chapter on The Poetics *in* Literary Criticism: A Short History *used other writing by Aristotle, such as his work on biology, to support* The Poetics. *In spite of this, do you find the vocabulary too limiting, an apparent copiousness?*

I'm not persuaded. I was a close personal friend and former student of Bill Wimsatt, but we always did enter into disputes from the day I was first his student to the time, alas, that he died. We never could agree on anything in terms of critical theory or critical practice. I think that I have always implicitly dissented from Aristotelian models, and now I would go further and say I would also dissent from Heideggerian and Hegelian models, which structuralism and post–structuralism, including the deconstructive wing of post–structuralism, are giving us. I don't believe in these philosophical models.

Stoic and Epicurean models in terms of philosophy, and Gnostic and Kabbalistic models in terms of religion, and which themselves owe a good deal I think to Stoic doctrines, are of more interest. The ancient critic that now interests me most is Crates of Mallos. He was the librarian at Pergamum when Aristarchus was at Alexandria, and there are various useful German books on his work. He was a powerful theoretician of rhetoric, and what he espoused was the mode of anomaly against the Alexandrian mode of analogy. That is to say, he was indeed interested in differences within texts and also intertextual differences. He used Stoic models of interpretation rather than the Alexandrian blend of Aristotelianism and Platonism.

There is certainly some relationship between Stoic modes of interpretation and the elements that develop into Gnostic exegesis like the Valentinian, such as Heracleon's exegesis of the Gospel of John. I find myself profoundly in sympathy with Gnostic modes of reading. I suppose I am strongly influenced by scholars like Hans Jonas and also by Gershom Scholem but also by an increasing acquaintance with Gnostic and Kabbalistic texts as well as with Stoic modes of interpretation, so that I am allowing myself to be found by my own tradition there. I think I have been doing this for some time, because there is an element of Stoic and indeed explicitly Epicurean mode of interpretation that does get into Pater very strongly, and before him does exist implicitly in Ruskin, and I would suppose that Ruskin, Pater, Wilde, and in this country, Emerson, who was a kind of intuitive Gnostic, are the major influences on my work.

What are the sources for Gnosticism now in print? Where can the commentary on John be found?

Heracleon was a disciple of Valentinus, and he left us an exegesis of the Gospel of John which is a Valentinian Gnostic interpretation. This, like most Gnostic texts, until those recently dug up at Nag-Hammadi, is preserved in various Christian heresiologists.

Why was the Gnostic system so viciously suppressed? What about it would so appall Christian ideology?

Oh, well, it appalled both Judaism and every orthodox variety of Christianity. It held that the creation was itself the fall, and that the true god was the abyss. Therefore from the very beginning it would have to be total anathema to both Judaism and Christianity. But quite clearly also it would lead to a very different aesthetic of creation.

Resembling Blake's?

Yes and no. Blake is a Gnostic in his view of nature but not in his view of man. He is half Gnostic and half anti-Gnostic. He is oxymoronic in that regard.

One of the reasons for asking about Blake is your use of Milton for several years as a model, partly through Blake's reading of Paradise Lost *and the view of Satan as demonic hero in that poem. These things do relate?*

Yes, they do relate, but it would be too difficult to adumbrate that, particularly as I'm increasingly uncertain, with Milton in particular, as to whether we have a way of talking about what it is that Milton is actually doing in *Paradise Lost*. I reject completely the orthodox accounts, but I have not yet found one to replace them.

Orthodox accounts such as those by C. S. Lewis?

Yes. All hopeless. All hopeless. Empson also is not the answer. Milton more even than Blake is an instance of someone who so persuasively redefines the tradition, including Christianity itself, that he makes it entirely in his image. He certainly in no way is Gnostic. He is anti–Gnostic, but his orthodoxy is such a powerful transumption of Christian orthodoxy, just as his classicism is such a transumption of the classical tradition, that we can only speak of the Miltonic. To call him a Christian poet is, I think, to beg the question in the extreme.

Could you say something more about your concept of the daemonic?

It's such a complicated concept. I suppose my major source for it is not what Goethe does with it, but with what the scholar E. R. Dodds does with it in *The Greeks and the Irrational*. That account of the daemonic seems to me the most plausible and useful that I've encountered.

Shelley refers to the creative demon, particularly as the "witch Poesy"—

Shelley uses daemon and demon more or less freestyle, substituting one for the other. I guess that I would also; *daemon* and *demon* are of course the same word, and I think it is wrong to try to divide them one from the other.

But of course it becomes very complex because there is the daemonic in the classical world and in Alexandria as expounded by Dodds, and there is the daemonic in European tradition which is a version of the sublime, or the *unheimlich* or uncanny, and Goethe is the *locus classicus* for the definition of it.

Do you think that traditional critical approaches are a mask to conceal cultural and literary differences?

What I think I have in common with the school of deconstruction is the mode of negative thinking or negative awareness, in the technical, philosophical sense of the negative, but which comes to me through negative theology. Gnosticism is the most extreme variety of negative theology that the West has ever known. But there is of course a great difference between the Hegelian negative, or the Nietzschean negative or the Heideggerean negative on the one side and the negative thinking that characterized Gnosticism or Kabbalah, or as I would say, poetic thought through the western ages.

Do you see anything that can provide a release from the self-consciousness that has grown, particularly in the twentieth century, about artistic creation? Among the many signs are T. S. Eliot's own criticism. . . .

There is no escape. It is simply the given, and there is nothing that we can do. In fact all we can do is keep increasing it, and this of course is where Hegel is the prophet. Hegel prophesied that this must finally mark the death of art, because this growing self-awareness, this growing self-consciousness must finally be destructive of the aesthetic.

It's entropic or an entropic ego?

Yes, it's entropic. Indeed, the three different prophesies about the death of individual art are, in their different ways, those of Hegel, Marx, and Freud. I don't see any way of getting beyond those prophesies.

I remember talking about this in *A Map of Misreading*. I guess that would express it as well as I could put it.

However, aren't you going beyond that definition of artistic limit
with your overt recognition of Gnosticism? Aren't you presenting
an alternative to the limits of self-awareness?

Not really. I wish I could believe that it was an alternative, but
as a negative theology and as a mode of interpretation, it is quite
desperately belated. It has the difficulty, that while I don't think it
is parasitic upon Judaism or Christianity or Platonism and Aristotelianism, nevertheless, as an anti-philosophy and as an anti-theology
it must regard, it must rely, to a very considerable degree in a way
that perhaps it is blind to, it must rely for its coherence partly upon
the world views that it has rejected. It is a very difficult question. I
think there has been both an implicit and explicit "Gnosticism,"
"Kabbalism," "occultism," from at least the High Renaissance to
the present.

Among poets, there has been a quite desperate reliance upon
such traditions as an attempt to evade just these matters we are
discussing. I do think that it does provide actual points of departure
and an alternative mode of interpretation, which means also an alternative mode of creation. But it is deeply marked. Its signature is
its belatedness, its——well, I'll use a phrase by Hans Jonas. It fascinated me because, even though I had read his works several times
before, I hadn't realized that in entitling an essay on Walter Pater
"The Intoxication of Belatedness" I had repressed my debt there to
Jonas. In the book *The Gnostic Religion,* which is the American
recension and revision of his earlier two volumes on *Gnosis and*
Ancient Times, he says that the Gnostics exhibited the "intoxication
of unprecedentedness." And of course, any intoxication of unprecedentedness is an intoxication of belatedness, because how can you
have this extreme ecstasy of unprecedentedness if you're not driven
to it by quite a desperate belatedness?

I suppose it's in that peculiar or particular sense that I would
bring forth the Gnostics of the first two Christian centuries as being
truly the first modernists. I would locate modernism in Alexandria
in the first two Christian centuries. It does not seem to me that there
has been much modification in literary or intellectual form. I am
going further back of course. I think you can see it coming up as
an intellectual or a literary and critical doctrine in second century B.C. Alexandria. That is to say before Roman literature, before

Christianity at all, before, even, the Palestinian modification of ancient Judaism which produces the rabbinical or normative tradition, there is, truly, the first modernism of the western world. There is the phenomenon of Hellenism in Alexandria. I think it's fair to say that everything that we deal with since is a kind of Hellenistic phenomenon, and what we call literature and what we call literary models are a Hellenistic manifestation. Insofar as you can pinpoint its birth in time, as good a point of departure as any other, as good a place to set up your axis, is Alexandria in the second century B.C.

Gnosticism itself is belated to that because it is a development of Hellenism and comes after Hellenistic culture itself had begun to be rather jaded. At least its cognitive, formal relations tend to be Alexandrian.

You read the Patristic writers?

Oh yes, including the heresiologists, like Irenaeus and Epiphanius, who are full of material.

So someone studying Gnosticism learns as much from the attacks on heresy as from the sources themselves?

The documents of the Gnostics we have acquired only relatively recently, and most of the texts with the exception of the Valentinian Gospel of Truth, which is a remarkable text, most are quite inadequate. They're not of the highest quality. They are far less interesting than the fragments of Gnosticism and the accounts of Gnosticism that one finds in the heresiologists.

There is, of course, also belated Jewish Gnosticism which is a very complicated story, because there was certainly an early Jewish Gnosticism, the texts of which we cannot recover, which were thrown outside. Mythology, Gnosticism, was thrown away by the rabbis of the first two centuries of the Christian era. There is, according to Scholem and others, some real connection historically between that early Jewish Gnosticism and the Kabbalistic transmission, which, however, does not emerge for one thousand years. It's not until the twelfth century or so, in Provence and then in Spain, that you have the Jewish nexus that gives us texts in the early Kabbalah.

You have discussed this in Kabbalah and Criticism?

Yes, there and elsewhere. I think that it can help make us even more aware and even more self-conscious of the critical and the poetic procedure, but it is not a way out of the dilemma. It is only a deepening of the dilemma.

You can agree, with the Lacanians, that the force of unconscious desire is what is going to perpetually preserve and save poetry, and with the deconstructionists or with Foucault that it is language itself which is its own guarantor of survival of the tradition. Language will go on. It will thus inevitably generate its own readings and misreadings and its own productivity.

I don't find that very persuasive at all.

It seems to me that there is inescapable diminishment, but it is dialectical diminishment because in that diminishment there are new shades of awareness which come to birth.

What about your novel, The Flight to Lucifer, *based on Gnosticism?*

Oh, I want to forget about it. If I could get it out of the libraries, I would. It is now out of print, and I would never do anything to bring it back. I think that I shall stick to writing literary criticism.

It was generally well reviewed, though I have heard the comment that it was more criticism than fiction.

A number of friends have said that. Well, what can I say. The very notion of a Gnostic fantasy, romance, or fiction is a very difficult notion, and it was not possible to write it without a very high degree of critical self-awareness.

The thing that could appear is the fact that any novel, any text, any record, is in part a fragment, is a contest of completion-incompletion.

Yes, that's true. There is a fascinating book by Thomas McFarland which is a theory of the fragment. I think that he's dealing with the theory as a literary genre in its own right. I don't know if he would go as far as I would, though I suppose he might.

I'm distinguishing here between the genre, the conceit, of the dis-

covered "fragment" that was a minor and calculated genre of the eighteenth century and later, and the aspect of all texts, no matter what their pretended completeness, that is nevertheless incomplete.

An adage to which I suppose everyone would subscribe to some degree is that a poem is not finished, it is only abandoned. Therefore in some sense—well, Shelley himself some time ago said language is the wreck of an abandoned cyclic poem, which I would still use as a sort of primary principle as to the proper relation between what language and poetry is. Of course, every cyclic poem is itself a fragment.

You have also said that there is no such thing as a poem in itself.

That's a sort of Nietzschean recognition, but even as there is no thing in itself, there is no such thing as a poet in himself or a poem in itself.

The completeness of all texts is a fiction, including of course the Gnostic texts and fragments?

Gnosticism is as much of a stance as it is a text. It is an interpretive mode which, partly by historical accident, of suppression, but partly by its very nature, is fragmentary.

Are not all poems, no matter what their emendation, no matter what their reliability in reflecting the authors' intentions, no matter what their notes, are they not all incomplete and partially fragmentary?

Sure.

Which then draws to them means of twentieth-century knowing such as Freudian analysis?

Yes, or any of the kinds of interpretation as demystification which see texts as being aggregations of differences rather than a unity. I would rely here upon the conception of the sublime in Longinus as being an *agon*. I favor an agonistic notion of culture, poetry, interpretation, of reading. I guess that insofar as I find a wavering center in my own work it would be the notion of the *agon*.

This includes more than the sense of contest?

I suppose that one of the basic texts for it in the modern period is Nietzsche's early text called "Homer's Contest with Hesiod," which in turn I think was deeply influenced by Burckhardt, who, in his studies of the Greeks, also emphasizes the concept of the agonistic, in which every Greek attempted to surpass one another and to surpass anteriority. That is at the heart of the Greek achievement. For Burckhardt, it is the essence of the Greeks, as it also is for Nietzsche, and I suppose I would agree.

In Gnosticism it's applied to God himself: that is to say, not the dualist vision of Manichaeism, of two, almost equally strong principles wrestling with one another, but of there being an *agon* between a so-called creative God who is seen as being a demiurge, or a botcher, and an original abyss.

You have brought these vocabularies and these approaches to American literature?

Emerson brought them to American literature.

When did you first notice that form and context in American letters?

Oh, I began to read Emerson intensely in 1963 or 1964. It was the reading of Emerson more than any other single factor which changed my writing and led to my formulation in the summer of 1967 of the characteristic notions that became the book *The Anxiety of Influence* and what came afterwards.

The peculiar assumption about American culture until recently was that it was innocent, that its surpassing of a former culture arrives at a new knowledge.

No. That is a very mistaken notion. It is a very knowing and has always been a very knowing and sophisticated way of realizing that you cannot arrive at a new knowledge.

One reading of Emerson, however, is precisely that defense of innocence, is it not? His essay on the American academy, the attack on the dependence on European learning—

I know, but I think that these are mistaken views of Emerson. Power "is in the shooting of a gulf," he says, "and in the darting to an aim"; it doesn't inhere in reaching the other side of that gulf or ending that darting process. Power in the agonistic sense is pretty clearly what Emerson understood.

The Gnostic approach to arrival, and completeness, or their opposites, this affects more texts than is admitted, even the canonized, supposedly complete texts in "definitive editions"?

All texts have this opposition. It is a self-negating element in the sense of temporal constructions, genealogies, mythologies, or fictions, and this has to do simply with the nature of language itself.

You still think though that Emerson is the *writer that one has to discuss and quote?*

In America, yes. He really is the fountainhead of our tradition. That really marks our difference from the Europeans. Though I must say, this is always misunderstood, but by now I'm so used to being misunderstood that I don't care any more.

However, aren't you more drawn toward the American pragmatists now?

No, no, no. I ran into this when I gave the Gauss lecture at Princeton. A scholar stood up and said, "You're really very naive, Mr. Bloom, that you think you can just use Peirce like this." I looked at him and said, "I'm not 'using' Peirce at all."

All that I'm taking out of pragmatism, whether William James or Charles Sanders Peirce or anybody else, is that sense Richard Rorty talks about, which is philosophical. And all I was taking out of Rorty was the very nice notion that it is perfectly silly for anybody to talk about criticism needing a philosophical foundation. It's rather like saying that the sciences should find their basis in the scriptures. Philosophy is dead. It's a stuffed bird. It's finished.

Isn't there a negative association with what you are saying? If literature is a preemptive discipline and philosophy is "dead," and we now live in a literary culture, it could be considered a decline of culture rather than an improvement.

I don't think Rorty is regarding it either as a decline or as an improvement. I'm not talking about it as a decline or an ascent either. I'm merely saying that's just the way it is, and it is anachronistic to go about saying that we must find a new rigor in our work, and that this rigor is determined by some philosophical antecedent or by some other outmoded dialectic. Philosophy is a totally dead subject. It is a stuffed bird on a shelf. So, of course, is religion, and they are equally dead and stuffed. Whatever literary criticism is or isn't, it makes as much sense to found it upon any mode of philosophy, whether it be Heideggerian or Peircean, or anything else, as it would be found on some specific theology, however negative.

I would again like to confront you with your notion of the agon. *How is it pertinent to artistic creation?*

But surely that is not necessarily unique with me. I can only repeat that both Burckhardt and Nietzsche quite accurately read the Greek spirit.

Nietzsche's great distinction is in *Zarathustra* when he says about the ancient Hebrews that they were the people whose central teaching was to honor their father and their mother, whereas the essential teaching of the ancient Greeks was to strive for the foremost place.

Art is not Hebrew, essentially. Western art is Greek. Therefore it does not honor its father and mother or even as our feminists would now have it, "Honor thy sister." Art always strives for the foremost place. If it doesn't strive for the foremost place, however implicitly, then whatever it is or isn't, it is not art.

The criticism, however, of your hypothesis is that it excludes more nurturing or "feminine" and less confrontational theories of artistic creation. You are criticized, for instance, in Madwoman in the Attic.

The first thing to do is to get rid of a very weak misreading of my theory, which is to say that I am basically applying an Oedipal model to the whole question of aesthetic creation. I do not think that I am applying an Oedipal model at all. I think I am looking at the matter as Longinus looked at it, or as Shelley did in *A Defense of Poetry* or insofar as I can tell, every major aesthetic consciousness in the history of the West has ever looked at it. To which I suppose many of the feminist critics would reply, well, because of male social constraints and male tyranny, and male brutality, these major aesthetic consciousnesses, with very rare exceptions, have been those of men rather than women. There's no reply to that, except to acknowledge, indeed, that the entire chain of male social brutality is immense and alas, not likely to cease.

I do notice that Elizabeth Bishop's poetry, when it is at its strongest, as it is in that great poem, "The End of March," she does not, even though I think she does in a remarkable passage near the close, consciously call in Miss Dickinson's "Presentiment—is that long Shadow—" to counter certain male exuberances of Mr. Wallace Stevens. But elsewhere in her work in ways she certainly couldn't have intended, as it were consciously, she undermines, or as I would say, transumes her friend and patroness, Marianne Moore, and her ultimate precursor Miss Dickinson of Amherst, as powerfully as she corrects or elaborates upon or transumes Mr. Wallace Stevens.

I find it fascinating to speak of a poet whose work I do not admire, the prophetess, the great shaman or shamanessa, Miss Adrienne Rich. I find it fascinating that in what is supposed to be a recent body of work which tries to establish itself in the true mode of the high feminist canon that there is scarcely a passage in which the actual poetic language consistently being struggled with is not that of another poet, on the whole one whom I do not greatly admire, the late Robert Lowell. That is to say, the old story is still being told. You learn to write in someone else's language, and then you struggle against it. In Miss Rich's generation, the rising poet, whether male or female, worked in various modes of Mr. Robert Lowell.

There are very good women poets writing now in America even with Miss Bishop dead and gone. The best of them, May Swenson— I'm speaking of the older generation, Miss Clampitt—in that same generation—Miss Sandra MacPherson and Miss Vicki Hearne in the younger generation (and again this has nothing to do with overt intentionality or design), it does seem to me that the struggle is very much that with precursors both male and female.

Most feminist poetry, of course, is like most black poetry. It isn't poetry. It isn't even verse. It isn't prose. It is just . . . I have no term for it. Maybe it is the cultural equivalent on one level of the literary criticism, say, of Mr. Hilton Kramer or Mr. Joseph Epstein, or Mr. Norman Podhoretz. These groups would not care for one another, but as demotic enterprises they have much in common. That is to say, they are all ideologues.

There are other forms of denatured Emersonianism.

Poor Ralph Waldo. The great problem for him has always been that he has either been literalized or weakly misread. All of this demoticism, of course, has the same relation to him or to the subtle, ineluctible, and very hermetic and very difficult and elitist poet, Walt Whitman, as I do to the moon.

What I mean is the insistence on the miniaturization of perception with an insistence on the self, the great ego, perceiving small moments of awareness—then writing about them. A lot of it was published in The New Yorker, *but it's seemingly everyplace.*

Yes, but that is nothing new.

Bad art always . . .

Yes, yes. Gresham's Law always works. Bad currency always drives out good. In any particular age, what you might call a middle level of decent work—critical, poetic, prose fictional—is always driven out by the whole flood of the demotic. But that's all right. It doesn't do any harm in the long run. What it always falls into in the end is what I would call Bloom's Law, which is the real point of what I call belatedness or that even incessant nonstop readers in the end must choose. They can spend only a certain amount of time reading and even less time rereading. The canon is not closed, as Ashbery or Thomas Pynchon are well able to evidence. There is always room for something really fresh and original.

What I've been calling belatedness I increasingly see as a question of how the temporal aspect of things has now produced a problem of demography. There are so many of us. There is real overpopulation. There is an overpopulation of texts, and there has been an extraordinary explosion of them. So you get a kind of increasing difficulty. I mean you can get a sect or a coven proclaiming that Nikki Giovanni or a lady who I gather is called Ai! A- I, or the Imamu Amiri Baraka, the ex LeRoi or The Emperor Jones, or Miss Rich, are poets of the highest splendor. Doubtless for ideological reasons—much abetted by W. W. Norton and Company in its various anthologies—they would have a certain number of readers for awhile, but these are not readers, of course. These are just dyslexiads.

The fundamental problem for authentic readers is always going to be how much time they've got to read and reread. If they are to keep themselves going they shall have to be rereading Shakespeare and Tolstoi and Proust, and Wordsworth, and Yeats, and Wallace Stevens, and so on. How much time can there be? And that, I believe in the end, except where you are dealing with a political or ideological matter, is going to determine things. You know, since so many of the feminist critics are women of a very high degree of education and intellect, feminist criticism is bound to improve. It will learn to make nicer and nicer distinctions.

I think it will finally have to confront the realization that its notion of sisterly cooperation between women writers is nothing but a noble idealization, because in the end it will hold as much even within these sects and covens as it does among whatever small body of adept or authentic readers we will have left. Whom does one read? How does one make the choice? Ultimately the reader of feminist poetry will have to say: Do I spend my time reading Emily Dickinson and Christina Rossetti and Amy Clampitt and Vicki Hearne or do I spend my time reading Ai or Miss Giovanni or Miss Rich or the late great Sylvia Plath?

What are you intending to write about Freud after your present project?

I am going to write a full-scale commentary of an exegetical sort on all of Freud's major writings. I feel that one does not exist. There is Richard Wollheim's *Sigmund Freud,* but it first of all doesn't have the necessary length to work in close. Also, Mr. Wollheim is a kind of Humean empiricist. Therefore, he keeps insisting that Freud has evidence of a sort for everything he says, which is quite untrue, of course. I just don't like any of the available commentaries, American, French, British, so I shall set out to de-esotericize and to write a needed book. Perhaps this is indicated in the tentative title, *Freud: Transference and Authority.* It shall be intended as a commentary on all of Freud's texts and will be without any special thesis to argue but with a deep urge to be normative and not esoteric. Surely it shall take me into areas that are bound to be controversial.

You have rejected the idea of Freud as a "scientist"?

Come, come, he's no scientist.

He writes in a metaphorical and hidden manner?

How are we going to go on deceiving ourselves in that regard? If Freud is science then Montaigne is science. Freud is exactly like Montaigne, and the figure in the twentieth century he is closest to is Marcel Proust. That is his only real rival in this century for someone who has vast literary and cognitive authority who writes.

I think we must say of Freud that after him there is only commentary. He has imposed an enormous facticity upon us, an enormous contingency. We are, now, as I have said so many times in print, all of us Freudians whether we want to be or not, the way people used to be Christians whether they wanted to be or not. The theology of the West, the normative psychology of the West, the mode of being of the West, is essentially Freudian, with a very small *f*.

One of the infallible manifestations of the Protestant evangelists and of the political right wing is that they so distrust psychology and psychoanalysis.

I would think so, because they can be so swiftly dispelled by the Freudian analytic. More sophisticated versions of contemporary belief of course cannot. But Freud would have dismissed those with a shrug as being impostors anyway.

So Freud when he was being most "scientific" was being most metaphorical?

Yes. He knew that. He says at the close of *Beyond the Pleasure Principle* that physics and all of the so-called exact or positive sciences always have to rely on trope or metaphor in order to say anything at all. He is well aware that his frontier concepts like *drive* and the *bodily ego* are nothing but tropes or metaphors. Cheerfully, he says that the language of science always has to be a figment of language. What else is there for it to be? He happens, of course, to be one of the most radically figurative authors ever to write.

What has led you to these revisions of Freudian dogma?

Teaching Freud for the last several years, I have become convinced that there is something most peculiar about the pattern of his work. The real crux in Freud is what happens in January 1912 when he simultaneously writes the first of the transference essays, that on "The Dynamics of Transference," and the second and fourth chapters of what will become *Totem and Taboo,* on "Taboo and Emotional Ambivalence" and "The Return of Totemism in Childhood." Then I think he dissimulated with us. I think he very clearly and knowingly models his account of the analytical transference upon his own mythopoeic account of totem and taboo: the analyst is of course the totem; taboo and transference are one and the same entity. I think this becomes the very center of his work and helps to account for the violent defenses, for the perfectly outrageous central myths or stories of *Totem and Taboo* throughout the rest of his life. It also accounts for the fact that he keeps rewriting *Totem and Taboo,* whether as *The Future of an Illusion* or *Moses and Monotheism,* or *Civilization and Its Discontents.* In short, I keep realizing that the most important page Freud ever wrote is that ghastly account of the primal history scene, the murdering and devouring of the totem papa by the primal horde, and that everything follows from this mad piece of mythological literalism.

The theory of the Oedipus complex is formulated after the book you are discussing?

No, no, it's formulated well before *Totem and Taboo,* back in the 1890s, just as the transference is formulated pragmatically long before it is conceptualized in January 1912.

When was Totem and Taboo *actually written?*

Most of it is written during 1912, the first of the cultural books to be published.

You have said that you consider Totem and Taboo *to be the most important of Freud's works.*

Yes, in terms of the pattern and the most important in terms of the development of his own work.

Your other point was that the poet and the critic owe very little to theories of the id, ego, superego?

Sure.

Isn't it confusing to have, at one point, the assertion that Totem and Taboo *should be established as a primary and formal pattern of Freudian theory, but that id, ego, and superego as a theory is secondary—*

No, it's not. I'm finding that I am abandoning the Freudian family romance as a paradigm for talking about the relationship between poets and am substituting the Freudian account of the dynamics of the transference, though not precisely the Freudian account, but what I think is the true account, which is the mythopoeic version given in the book, *Totem and Taboo*. I guess that I would go even further. What Freud and the Freudians call countertrans ference, but are not able to write about and choose not to write about, now seems the best model for what I call influence anxiety.

So you plan to complete the book on Freud after your series for Chelsea House, the "Modern Critical Views"?

Yes, if I ever finish that editorial work! Remember what my greatest precursor Dr. "Schmuel" Johnson said: No man but a blockhead would write for anything except money.

But you know, in the end I would say that the difference between myself and all other contemporary literary critics who have reputations or who are considered to be of some note is this: what I'm having a chance to do by writing five hundred introductions short and long is that I don't have any trouble now in writing these introductions in such a way that a fair number of them can just be taken by Barbara Epstein of the *New York Review of Books* and can be printed for a general literate public. It does seem to me that that kind of criticism was written by Samuel Johnson in *The Lives of the Poets,* and *The Rambler,* and "The Preface to Shakespeare," and even in *Rasselas.* It was what was written by William Hazlitt every day of his life no matter what his ostensible subject was. It is what is written endlessly in Ruskin.

This motive of criticism sets aside what Geoffrey Hartman keeps urging on us with his battle cry that criticism must be creative. I can only say that some of it is going to be, some of it isn't, but it is always a genre or subgenre of literature. What else can it be? It isn't a human science, it isn't an exact science, it isn't necessarily a pedagogical skill or adjunct. If it's memorable, then it has to pass the test it has always passed. Certainly it doesn't have to be written by poets: Hazlitt was not a poet, the sublime Walter Pater was not a poet, and the divine Oscar Wilde wrote the world's worst poetry. So whether criticism survives as a subgenre of literature really has to do with the question of why we can still read a lot of Hazlitt or Dr. Johnson. They are not only remarkable representatives of a particular time. They are experiential. They are wisdom writers.

I think that those who get involved in polemics and write books saying that criticism should be creative are off on the wrong track. I don't think that's the issue nor should it be. While there are "creative" critics, there are never very many of them, and the academy is certainly very unhappy about them. But to say that criticism should be creative is another issue entirely. As with everything else in life, it either is or it is not. Most criticism whether of a newfangled kind or an oldfangled kind is just not creative at all. But then, most poetry is not creative at all, including a great deal of celebrated contemporary poetry.

In a review of Isaac Rosenberg's collected work, you mention that American Jewish poets have yet to establish a strong, independent identity.

Yes, there's a lack of independence, of autonomy. I don't know if I'm hard on it, just that it so happens that so far very little really strong, first-rate work has been done by Jewish poets or on Jewish subject matter, whatever that is. I think Rosenberg in his best five or six poems is as good a poet as one could find if he were looking for a Jewish poet writing in English. But he's very minor. It just so happens, I can't explain it, that of the dozen or so American poets so far in this century, none happens to be Jewish. There are very good poems by John Hollander, or by Philip Levine, and there are good poems by Irving Feldman and others—the situation may change, but up to now it just isn't very good.

What reactions have you had to your statements about this?

Oh, nastiness, terrible nastiness on the part of poets, their friends, and their relatives. But, you know, I usually get nasty reactions anyway. I can't afford to let it bother me, and by now it doesn't bother me. But I think it has become a kind of automatic even knee-jerk reaction to what I do.

You have had some interesting exchanges with Cynthia Ozick?

I admire her writing and the exuberance of her personality. In fact we have met only twice in this life, once at our now more or less celebrated debate at the Jewish Museum several years back, and once when she was kind enough to come to a talk I gave in Jerusalem. We exchange an occasional letter, but we both agree now that we have, as they used to say, buried the hatchet and are chums.

So you are no longer the villain of Art and Ardor?

I notice in a recent *Washington Post* article about me from August 20, 1985, that Cynthia gets in a parting shot when she says, skipping her various exalted compliments to me, that I lack "Jewish information." At which point one has to ask, how is the distinguished Ms. Ozick using that much abused word *information*? She's certainly not using it in the very interesting sense used by my friend, the great poet John Ashbery, when he asks the question, "*Was* it information?" in "Soonest Mended," or when he implicitly answers that question in the equally powerful "Wet Casements," where he says, not having a particular name and vital phone number of some overheard individual at a party: "I want that information very much today, / Can't have it, and this makes me angry." So I really don't know what Cynthia means by a "lack of information." It could appear to be a lack of the proper reverence for Normative Judaism.

I think it is not a major sorrow of the Jewish people at this time, because their major sorrow is that they go on having so many enemies, but certainly it is a sign of the general Western cultural malaise, or Western religious malaise, that, to use the phrase of Norman Podhoretz or Hilton Kramer or Joseph Epstein, any "elitist intellectual"—which you might just as well translate as thoughtful and sensitive reader and thinker or just experiencer of the Jewish persuasion—can these days convince herself or himself that the glowing moral fossil of the second century of Common Era Judaism, Normative Judaism, is relevant or applicable to the spiritual necessities of being alive in the 1980s.

So Ozick by Jewish *means Normative Judaism?*

She means Normative Judaism. When she called me an anti-Jewish critic, which is unfortunate, as she might now agree, it's the only thing that made me angry because it is so subject to misunderstanding. Neither Bloom nor Ozick by "anti-Jewish" means what is vulgarly or commonly called "anti-Semitism."

It goes without saying, but I'm going to say it anyway: if Judaism is in bad condition today, that which passes for Christianity anywhere in the world would of course be in at least as bad condition if not considerably worse. But that's not my concern. That doesn't interest me in the slightest. It is a deep puzzle to me and it's an interesting lesson I've been slowly trying to teach myself all my life, namely, the uses of misprision, of misreading. Normative Judaism is an extremely strong misreading of the Hebrew Bible which was done eighteen hundred years ago to cover the needs of the Jewish people in Palestine under Roman occupation. Since the Jewish people either live in a Palestine that is not exactly under the occupation of the Roman Empire or live in the Western world or live in bondage in the Soviet Union—in whatever conditions they live in one place or another—that powerful and very strong misreading in the second century of the Common Era strikes me as very fascinating and well worth consideration. But the notion that it should in any way bind me as the proper version of the covenant is ridiculous.

So what's the proper or primary reading on which this "misreading" occurred?

Well, it all depends on whether you would accept the notion of the chain of tradition, of the chain of authorized interpretation in each generation as it is set forth, say, at the opening of one of the great texts of this tradition, the Ecclesiasticus, of the Jesus Ben Sirach, the remarkable Old Testament and so-called Apocrypha which includes the famous passage, "Let us now praise famous men and our fathers that begat us." That passage is a definite expression of the chain of tradition and is closely related to an even more magnificent passage at the opening of the Ethics of the Fathers, or The Sayings of the Fathers, the Pirke Aboth, the most astonishing tractate of the Talmud, which is the statement that the Torah was given to Moses, was transmitted by him to the men of the Great Synagogue. The so-called Academy of Ezra flows through this or that authorized group until it reaches its culmination in the very grand group of readers whom we regard as the great Rabbis of the second century of the Common Era centering around Akiba and Tarfon and Ishmael and their colleagues.

But of course the whole thing is so complex. They took themselves to be, or at least modern scholarship takes them to be, and of course modern Normative Judaism takes them to be, the direct continuators of the Pharisees. But the differences between first century Judaism and second century Judaism are so great that I'm not persuaded that there is a direct ongoing flow from the major Pharisees to the great expositors surrounding Akiba in the second century. What is clear is that for eighteen hundred years now, the formulation worked out in Roman Palestine by Akiba and Ishmael Ben Elisha and the others has been the staple of Judaism ever since.

I suppose that what principally interests me about this is that I have slowly and patiently during the past six or seven years been rereading those portions of Genesis, Exodus, Numbers, which modern scholarly tradition rightly attributes to the "J writer" or Yahwist. The more deeply I read in them, I have the same experience that I have when I read in Shakespeare and to a lesser extent the more deeply I read in Freud, which is that the radical originality of that primordial author of the three books that we now call Genesis, Exodus, Numbers is in effect so great, so overwhelming, that what he or she or it has to say about the nature of God or the nature of the covenant or the nature of history or human personality or anything else has almost nothing to do with the entire history of subsequent revision, whether a century later with the Elohist or a little bit further on with the so-called priestly school, or with the whole movement after the return from Babylon, the Great Synagogue or Academy of Ezra. Indeed even long before that, what prophetic tradition made of the Yahwist has very little to do with the Yahwist as I read the Yahwist, who is still the strongest writer ever to write in the Hebrew language.

There is not the slightest relation between what his text is offering us and anything in the tradition afterward. That is what I find most interesting and most appalling about the whole problem. But of course, I've been accused of trading in the controversial for its own sake, but I don't suppose that when I do find the time, the knowledge, and the energy to write a book on this whole matter, that there is anything I have ever written or said that will cause as much nastiness to fall upon me as this will. Indeed, I've already had such bad experiences addressing Jewish groups both here and in Israel on the whole question of Jewish culture or Jewish texts that I will not again address such groups.

Would you clarify the phrase "Normative Judaism"?

The phrase was used by the great Harvard scholar of religion Mr. George Foot Moore in describing the Judaism of the second century and that which has prevailed since. It is a brilliant description. It's a great term for it. I see that a number of Jewish scholars have adopted it.

Yes, but isn't Judaism doing well in the United States?

Yes, but what has this to do with matters of the intellect or the spirit? What is one to say? My concern obviously is not with all of these activities. They are socially and in a familial way beneficent, but what is the intellectual and spiritual content of American Judaism? I would say at this time that it is about as flatly unimpressive as the intellectual or spiritual content of American Roman Catholicism or American Protestantism of any variety, whether liberal or fundamental. That I regard as a scandal.

But one can go further. I think that the real sadness of Jewish life in America once you get away from its societal or organizational aspect, is to contrast the American Jews with let us say German-speaking Jewry of sixty or seventy years ago before Hitler and the

Holocaust. For all of the profound tangles and contradictions, the psychic and spiritual agonies of those Jewries, they were, as we all know, enormously productive. But what am I offered as they were culturally? The cultural or spiritual productivity of American Jewry? Norman Podhoretz? Joseph Epstein? Hilton Kramer? I mean what is this? Traditional Jewish scholarship is strong in the United States. But I find this recent phenomenon of the whole new generation of younger scholars in Jewish Studies or Judaic Studies, mushrooming up all over the landscape in departments in American universities, a dubious entity indeed. It is an attempt, I suppose, to make more accessible and attractive to current American undergraduates the whole traditional bric-a-brac of the remnants of the normative. But it seems to me threadbare and unlikely to do more than perhaps furnish a little mental furniture for people who need some mental furniture. But this opinion too is only going to make a fresh packet of nonadmirers. Everyone must be aware of this: there can hardly be an American college or university with any pretensions which does not have a sort of Jewish Studies or Judaic Studies bit going. But there's nothing at the core of it.

Again, if you say that there is a decline, what is the standard you are using?

The trinity I keep thinking of is the three who, for better or worse, have nothing, absolutely nothing in common with the normative tradition. I mean if you think of Jewish culture in the twentieth century and you think of the foremost names, there is no question that for "intellectual elitists," as the *Commentary* gang would call them, there is Sigmund Freud, there is Franz Kafka, and there is Gershom Scholem. All the three have in common is that what they would have regarded as their relation to Jewish tradition has absolutely nothing in common with Normative Judaism.

What then have you to say about the current state of Israel?

I have nothing to say. Of course I am absorbed, interested, and full of sympathy, but I have nothing to say.

It's not possible to be upset with politics in contemporary Israel?

Who can be upset? One just wants Israel to survive.

What has happened to the old German liberal and socialist political stance of the founders?

I think that's over, but I don't think that this neoconservative Epstein, Podhorrors, and Hilton Kramer jazz involves more than a handful of people. The Jews of America like all other upper middle class Americans—I mean that's it—are now indistinguishable from the other upper middle class Americans. They have blent in, and if the country goes through a Reaganite phase, they will be Reaganites. If after Reagan the country moves mildly back to slightly left of center, instead of being to the right of center, then they will go along with that also.

But, you know, the election of '84 was fascinating in one regard. This Podhoretz gang aside, Reagan got every other part of the white electorate except for the Jewish vote. He didn't get it only, I am convinced, because of those last minute intimations that he shared the Jerry Falwellian obsession with "The Rapture"—as they call it— the notion that the atomic holocaust was going to come in our time and in this rather peculiar literalizing of that dreadful text, The Revelation of John the Divine, that the state of Israel would have to be incinerated in order for the blessed Jesus to reappear. After which all of us, Mr. Reagan, Mr. Falwell, and all the rest of us were going to be gathered up in "The Rapture."

I think that was a bit much for the Jewish electorate.

You follow the Christian evangelists?

They fascinate me. In fact, they are now my favorite television entertainment. If I cannot find old movies of real interest to watch, I simply sit there rapt in front of the night's worth of evangelists, admiring their different rhetorical styles, the nice points of their doctrines.

What all of them demonstrate is how right Freud was, as I've already said, about the close relations between repressed or displaced sexuality and religion. He insisted it was the longing for the father. You frequently have the notion that he must be slightly mistaken, but only slightly, because clearly it is a longing for the poppa *and* the momma.

Actually, the most original version of an American theology of a fundamentalist kind, and I always tell this to my classes in American literature, I saw some years ago when a lady who is still extant, Jane Russell, teamed up with a couple of other ladies more or less in their Hollywood decline. They got very evangelical. They had all gotten converted, and they would come on and sing gospel songs rather badly. On one occasion the interlocutor asked Miss Russell what her idea of God was. With a marvelous kind of Texas enthusiasm, she proclaimed—and I believe this is a verbatim quotation— she said, "I think God is just a livin' doll." Isn't that wonderful?

I think that entitles her to very high rank among contemporary fundamentalist theologians in the United States. Ah, Yahweh, how thou art fallen from thyself! Thou hast become a livin' doll!

In spite of what you just said about TV religion and what you wrote in Vogue *magazine, why are you such an unrelenting critic of what is called "high culture," and do you intend to remain so?*

You must mean my 1985 review in *Vogue* of *Family Album* by the writer who is called Danielle Steel? I had never read anything by that writer before, but I read every word of the proof copy of *Family Album*. I came to the conclusion that there may not actually be a Danielle Steel, that it must be a combine or a computer which works by formula, very successfully indeed.

But concerning "high" culture. There is no other. Everything else is a compost heap. It has been and always will be.

But has it ever been really different? I think Eric Havelock is quite right. Homer could be high, middle, and low culture simply because you didn't have literacy. You had to rely on memory and you had to rely on it for an oral recitation. Therefore you got the Platonic polemic against Homer. But since we now do what we call communications so differently . . . but I really don't see any change. Alfred Lord Tennyson and Robert Browning are astonishingly great poets. So I believe are John Ashbery and James Merrill. The only difference that I can see is that Browning and Tennyson were different in this: what did they have to compete with? They had to compete with the Protestant churches, and with the three volume novel—and to some extent the popular press.

But of course, we haven't just television. We've got rock and we've got videotape. You know the other day, I looked at my friend Frank Lentricchia's book called *Criticism and Social Change,* which seems to me a very courageous attempt to make a case for something which I find wholly absurd, whether it is presented by out-and-out Marxist critics, or a modified one like Frank. He was making the case that it doesn't really make any difference if you are Walter Pater or T. S. Eliot, and I think implicitly in the end the case was being made against me, you know, that Pater's elitism is the elitism of a social class. But that cuts no ice with me. Western literature increasingly has got to be the province, precisely because of this quite Hellenistic or Alexandrian phenomenon of belatedness, it's got to be the interest or the concern or the province of those who have had, indeed, an elitist and therefore (and I am delighted to say this in the Oscar Wildean sense), a *decadent education.* It has to be education more in the Augustan mode than in the high Romantic. Alexander Pope I increasingly see as the patron saint of whatever true elite we have left, rather than William Wordsworth. This is not to say ultimately of course that Wordsworth is not a more influential poet, magnificent as Pope was, because what can elitist culture be at this time, whether it be a literary culture or whether it be some other version of high culture? What can it be but the refinement and the elaboration and the conservation of what can still be conserved? It's got to hold onto whatever canon it can hold onto in the face of social assaults of the most ignorant kind, whether they mask themselves as a Third Worldism, Fourth Worldism, neo-Feminism, or some other coven, sect or evangelicanism, or ideologies of every sort, including the entire French wave.

French Freud?

It really isn't French Freud of course. It's French Heidegger. I mean the one thing I think that Lacan and Jacques Derrida and Deleuze and all of these fellows have in common is that they are all of them misreadings, whether strong or weak, of Heidegger. Therefore what they give us is not Freud but Heidegger. But I don't know why we need French Heidegger. German Heidegger is doubtless more than enough.

What were we saying about the French invasion? It of course is by now a dead issue. I notice that it is moribund even here at

Yale, which is supposed to be a citadel. But of course you know how these phenomena work. Long after it has died, it will keep emanating, so that it will be hot in Davenport for a long time to come, which is not an attack on the great city of Davenport, but it's just the way these things always go. Everybody's always belated in reference to something.

Why Heidegger and literature? What's the nexus?

Oh, the interesting part of Heidegger is surely the earliest, the first part of *Sein und Zeit*. That is the Heidegger who performs what he calls *destruction,* which in Jacques Derrida's misreading becomes deconstruction. And Paul de Man was even more Heideggerian than Jacques is. But I think there has been a mixup. What passes for a straight Heideggerian criticism in the United States really gets all mixed up with the fact that a lot of Heidegger is really an overt paraphrase of Hölderlin and has to do with his own variety of what is a rather unwholesome theology. It is, you know, another survivor of evangelical pietism in the German tradition. All of this presumes, of course, that you can read Heidegger at all. It's not the linguistic difficulty. It's just that Heidegger is hard as hell to read.

To conclude, I did want to ask you about Hilton Kramer, whom you mentioned earlier.

Hilton Kramer is a very minor league survivor of what you might call the Hugh Kenner version of literary modernism of which the high priests are T. S. Eliot and to a lesser extent Ezra Pound. Kramer is merely a lower middle brow literary journalist who is another survivor of the fringe of what was called the New Criticism in America—you know, the criticism of Allen Tate and Cleanth Brooks.

I owe Kramer a great debt though. Some years ago, when I was still an obscure esotericist and he was an art critic and an occasional columnist in the Sunday *New York Times Book Review,* he devoted an entire page to what he called the triumph of misreading at Yale in which I was the culprit. He clearly evidenced that he didn't know the difference between what I was calling misreading and what de Man was calling misreading and *plain dyslexia.* The poor fellow thought that I was recommending or advocating a kind of deliberate dyslexis.

However, Kramer did me a lot of good. He brought forth a flood of letters and much controversy. The sales of my books zoomed upwards. Sweet are the uses of journalism!

I think the best thing ever said about him is said by a novelist whom I increasingly admire to some extent as a novelist because of *Myra Breckinridge* and *Lincoln,* but particularly as a social critic and literary commentator, Mr. Gore Vidal, who invariably in print and in oral discourse refers to Mr. Kramer as "The Hotel Hilton Kramer."

You could of course ask me about Mr. Joseph Epstein of Chicago, the proud editor of that which passes for the magazine which dares to call itself with the honorific Emersonian title *The American Scholar,* who in a review of *Art and Ardor* by Miss Ozick, remarked that he wondered why Miss Ozick bothered to try to deal with a totally unreadable critic. Mr. Epstein is what my friend John Hollander would call "a good speller." That is, he can just about read without moving his lips.

I think that is the real issue in all of this. I don't want to say that my enemies are also the enemies of others—therefore this makes the others my friends. But in that general blanket attack upon the Franco-Heideggerians, all Podhoretz, Kramer, and Epstein manifest is their total lack of cognitive ability. Not to know the difference between a perfectly Emersonian idea of reading like my own and the Franco-Heideggerian notion of reading is to show indeed that these fellows never read at all.

Well, they *can* move their lips. They can evidently read the editorial page of the *New York Times.* Yes, at that level.

READINGS

Harold Bloom's *Shelley's Mythmaking* (1959) and *Poetry and Repression* (1976) were published by Yale University Press. *Blake's Apocalypse* (1963) and the commentary for *The Poetry and Prose of William Blake,* edited by David Erdman (1965) were published by Doubleday. Seabury Press was the publisher for *Figures of Capable Imagination* (1976) and *Kabbalah and Criticism* (1975), and

Oxford University Press published *Yeats* (1970), *The Anxiety of Influence* (1973), *A Map of Misreading* (1975), and *Agon* (1982); Cornell University Press, *The Visionary Company* (1961) and *Wallace Stevens* (1977); University of Chicago Press, *The Ringers in the Tower* (1959) and *The Breaking of the Vessels* (1982). *The Flight to Lucifer: A Gnostic Fantasy* (Farrar, Straus & Giroux, 1979) is Bloom's only novel. He is the editor of *Romanticism and Consciousness* (W. W. Norton, 1970) and an editor of *The Oxford Anthology of English Literature,* Volume II (1973). His already published and forthcoming editions of criticism on major American and British writers are published by Chelsea House, and he writes regularly for *The New York Review of Books*. A collection of Bloom's recent criticism, *Poetics of Influence,* has been edited, with an introduction, by John Hollander (Henry Schwab, 1986).

GEOFFREY HARTMAN

You have been a persistent critic of literature, writers, and kinds of style. In a review on Roland Barthes, you complain about the way literature is taught, or even viewed in the United States. What did you mean by that?

I'm not sure that I complain about it. I show that there is a difference of traditions. In the case of Anglo-American criticism or style of thought as it has developed through the academy, there is a greater emphasis on a certain kind of pedagogical decorum. Whereas in Europe, although that is a large generalization, there seems to be more flexibility in terms of audience or style of thought. Clearly, there is a university style in Europe, too, in German, Swiss, and French universities. A pedagogical style, expository, introductory, and so forth, but there is also another level, which in England and the United States would come out as journalistic or free-lance. Although it might be tied to academic issues, there is in Europe a greater freedom of style, orders of discourse, let's say.

Twenty or thirty years ago it was thought, perhaps inaccurately, that

the new critics then at Yale, such as Cleanth Brooks, were doing the
same thing as explication. *How does their explication of a text differ*
from the European sense of the term?

The phrase *explication de texte* is obviously French, and the
thing itself was and continues to be a staple of French educational
pedagogy at the secondary level and even in the university. It was
founded on the increased philological and historical knowledge of
the nineteenth century which is not only a French but also a German
achievement. But, as always, the French managed to fashion a relatively urbane public style in these matters of education, and they
carried it over into *explication,* which is just a useful way of com-
municating and releasing stored knowledge through the study of
selected texts. It's a good technique, but it did not have to raise
matters of theory. It was a practical instrument, tacitly imbued with
ideological and historical preconceptions. It simplified history, but
it did acculturate the student.

The explication of the New Criticism, while it obviously shares
text-centeredness, tries not to introduce historical, biographical, or
certain other orders of what it calls extrinsic fact into the analysis
of texts. It brackets these or excludes them without denying their
value; it only denies their value at this point in the procedure. It
thinks that it can gain a clear sense of texts and perhaps a fairer
and juster estimate of them without the premature and in-digest use
of these highly charged and ambiguous facts.

Do you think that this is a ruse? Brooks has a well-known essay on
Marvell's Horatian Ode *to Cromwell which relies heavily on his-*
torical citations—not to everyone's satisfaction. The New Critics do
move back and forth. Don't they inevitably mix history and critical
annotation?

Well, admitting the differences, one might say that Socrates has
his ruses. The Socratic Method—it's a ruse, but justified by the
pedagogical aim. I am no longer sure what someone like Brooks, or
Wimsatt, who is a very deep historical scholar, would have *said*
concerning the nature and function of historical knowledge. But in
some way they would have justified it. The question is one of decorum and utility at that stage. The critic as a kind of guide should
have that knowledge: That he should exercise restraint and withhold

\

it, yet try to achieve an interpretation or an induction of the student up to a certain point, says nothing against the method.

The problem is, where do you get to, and is there a particular, linear or progressive point at which you *must* introduce historical questions? Or is this the wrong kind of view because historical issues are always operative? So it's a question of method, in part, and secondly, it introduces the whole matter of whether the student is not put under some kind of charm or illusion which, while it may be beneficial to a point, finally makes him too puristic and restricts him so that questions of theory never come up.

You may remember that I. A. Richards, the father of the term "practical criticism," when he writes the book entitled such, does not write it in order to set practical criticism against theory but as a provocation to theory. He points out that nowhere is there less theorizing than in literary criticism. He says even football, soccer, has more theory to it, and practical criticism is to lead one into the perplexities that one encounters, into the problematic of the subject, in the hope that more thought be given to questions arising out of what practical criticism manifests.

Now it's ironical that as practical criticism developed in America, we find an exclusion of theory or of criticism dealing with theoretical questions. We find a kind of American isolationism that includes, increasingly, an isolation from continental currents. For on the continent this sort of isolation never really occurred, and *explication de texte* in France is just a miniature encyclopedic process.

Another question concerning Brooks. One of his essays published on T. S. Eliot's The Waste Land *does reveal a method—*

Oh yes. A relative disinterestedness in theory doesn't exclude methods. What Brooks has, though, is less method than tact and decorum. The method is a negative one. It's hygiene. It's hygienic criticism, and part of that hygiene is certainly based on a sense of limit derived from social events, taboos, religious scruples. In general, what does one tell people and what does one not tell? What does one speak about and when? If there are children, how much does one tell them? I think this is very deep in Brooks.

It's interesting that you choose Brooks because it's deeper in him, perhaps, than in Warren, who is a novelist, and much freer, or in Wimsatt, though there are obviously interesting restraints in Wimsatt too.

Are the restraints those of conventional Christianity?

It has turned out to be so. That is, one would have guessed it was, knowing the background of Brooks and Wimsatt. The evolution of their work, especially Brooks's work, has brought this more into the open. However, I don't know what you mean by traditional Christianity since there are so many types. What is traditional? But it may be that it is a Christianity that has blended itself with a social decorum.

I mean Protestantism, of course, but beyond that the fear of schism.

That might be true in the case of Brooks. Wimsatt was Catholic, was always argumentative, and even enjoyed the idea that there might be schismatics in the academy. He would take on anyone, would force them, in fact, to declare themselves. Wimsatt's decorum was quite different; he was always at the edge of intense and apocalyptic thoughts about decadence, of the "center not holding," of original sin.

I remember during the heady, apocalyptic days of the late 1960s that in an article I had published in *Yale French Studies* he came across (probably not for the first time, but this signaled to him) Kafka's little parable about the leopard's entering the temple and drinking the sacrificial chalices dry. They do it again and again, and finally it is made part of a ceremony. It can be reckoned on beforehand. Wimsatt was struck by that parable. It represented to him things that were happening. He saw the leopards at the gate and he saw myself, and even more, Harold Bloom, as allowing this kind of movement into the academy, into the temple, and trying to incorporate it in a way he felt was illegitimate. He didn't want the tigers to drink the sacrificial chalices dry. He wanted the sacrificial chalices here and the tigers out there. He wanted no confusions of that sort.

I guess they were leopards rather than tigers, and the essay was called "The Day of the Leopard." I had read it in a first version, where he cited my comments on that parable. He put them in a montage with all kinds of newspaper statements—really inflammatory quotations.

I said to him, "Look, aren't you sinning against your own principle of confusing literature, something in Kafka, with something the critic says, and journalistic statements?" I tried to catch him on his own principle of order.

But the exchange showed his state of mind, that of an extremely deep-feeling and honest person. He was one of the two to whom I dedicated *The Fate of Reading*. And he did modify his essay—I don't know whether it was a result of our conversation. He made it much fuller and less centered on my discussion of Kafka. I admit I have some qualms on rereading the end of my own essay because it deals with the subject of transgression too easily.

In something that Bloom wrote, *The Breaking of the Vessels*, one sees the sacrificial chalices being broken. But you can only break the vessels once, whereas the tigers, leopards, or whatever, can come in and drink them dry again and again. There is a kind of order by repetition that is suggested.

You mentioned Warren in passing. What is your relation to his criticism?

Very little. I think he is important through several first-rate essays. He is obviously a fine thinker, a fine writer. He could have been, perhaps, the most important of these critics, but he had other things to do, his poetry and his fiction. Essays like those on "Pure and Impure Poetry," and on the "Ancient Mariner" are important because they reflect a debate of the 1930s we have lost sight of, concerning the notion of "pure" poetry as it came via the Symbolists. He did make an interesting contribution, though his actual engagement with the "Ancient Mariner," while complex for that time, is not so complex, actually, for our time. But that's how criticism moves. Nonetheless, it is important because he picks up, very sensitively, the question of pure and impure poetry, which also figures largely in a forgotten book, "forgotten" I mean by most people, Frederick Pottle's *The Idiom of Poetry*, which takes up that question. It is a splendid book which appeared in 1941.

This is a slightly different direction from the other questions, but what did Pottle represent that departed from the Boswellian and the Johnsonian school, the biographical approach to literature? He cer-

tainly didn't fall in the same category as the metaphor of property management implied in books like Tinker's The Good Estate of Poetry.

Pottle had such an interesting personal career that one should really do a biography of Boswell's biographer.

While he is now known as a scholar-biographer of the eighteenth century, wasn't his first mark made in writing about the English Romantics?

His first love was science and he had a cold genius for description. He went from science through some genial-alchemical process to Shelley and Shelley's own interest in science. Through Shelley, then, he expanded into the Romantics, but Shelley of course is not simply a Romantic, whatever that means. He gathers into himself certain elements of the Enlightenment. Let's put it this way—he also belongs to the eighteenth century.

It's a very complex thing with Pottle. He never really separated the biographical and the literary. He could do both. I think he never felt a great tension between them. He, I don't think, was overly concerned with pedagogical questions at all. He's just a different kind of person who, however, supported the New Criticism in what it tried to do. He saw that it was an intelligent movement.

The impression that one has of the period before the New Criticism is that it is heavily historical, particularly Protestant, about the issues arising from the seventeenth century in England, the new consciousness of the power of language, of liberty, which are later represented in such books as David Masson's writing on Milton in the nineteenth century. Milton was a poet but as importantly was a specimen of a Protestant consciousness. So before the pretext of attention to textual primacy, there was a very heavy and somewhat literal reading of literature as Christian apologetic. Now, did Brooks really look more closely at the text or is his textual attention merely a disguise?

Well, *there* is a difficult question, the relation of the academic establishment to religious habit or discipline. Too much could be said about this, and you are right to see a relation. Coleridge saw it and talked about a Clerisy, and there is no question that, socially speaking, the academy, especially as it expanded toward undergrad-uate education in America, tried to transfer some of the religious and evangelical function to itself. That was a very natural thing. I don't think it was a conspiracy or even all that deliberate.

Concerning Milton: both he and Shelley were embattled figures in modern criticism, Milton because he did represent a radical de-velopment within Protestantism which, instead of eliminating or by-passing literature, reinforced it. Whereas one would have thought if Milton had been a more literal Puritan it would have worked the other way.

Shelley is interesting because of what could be interpreted as a conspicuous displacement of religious enthusiasm to poetry, and Pottle wrote against Leavis and others a most important article called "The Case of Shelley." I never took courses with Pottle. Har-old Bloom did, and his thesis came out of that tutelage or worked within and against it.

Figures such as Milton and Shelley are a field of force competed for by literature and religion when they appear to separate.

One more question regarding this—one may repeatedly note the quest for unity in academic criticism. M. Sofie Røstvig, for instance, insists that Marvell's poem to Fairfax is a work of unity. Kathleen Coburn maintains that there is unity in Coleridge's Biographia Lit-eraria. *Brooks, again, talks about the unity that one derives from* The Waste Land. *Isn't this a very heavily imposed construct?*

Yes, it is.

Now why is this?

You already mentioned the avoidance of schism. I'm not sure the principle of unity comes out of Christianity, but it may enter Protestant poetics from the religious wars, and it is like a faint conceptual echo of those bloody issues.

I would expand that and say that if one were to make a his-torical study of these things, the lines of force are clear. The problem with historical study is in its minute articulations, what Marxist criticism calls "mediations." It can be asserted that criticism be-comes a *via media* discourse, like so much in England.

As in Locke and his numerous imitators?

Exactly. We don't have much before 1600 because we don't have much prose criticism. You must have prose as a medium. Maybe prose as a medium reflects this curious blend of urbanity, a certain mixture of classes, the avoidance of extremes of "enthusiasm."

But there had to be two events to make the trauma (I'm using metaphors now) that led to the defense called the *via media*. One is the religious wars of the sixteenth century culminating in the establishment of the Tudors, and then the reopening of the issue with Cromwell—and so work back to Marvell's poem. Marvell plays an important part here in terms of poetic decorum. The wound opens again with the Civil War, and this time it is the extreme of Puritanism, not the extreme of Catholicism, that is defended against. This second opening in a sense seals the trauma, and many things, Swift's dislike of enthusiasm, the general eighteenth-century gentlemanly establishment . . .

The "country house"?

That's right. The ethos certainly goes back to that. Why it should have transferred itself, why it should have been given a new life in the 1930s is an interesting question.

The crisis in England occurred again during the French Revolution, but what in America is comparable during the twentieth century?

There must have been something. It's too difficult because America went through its own civil war, but I suppose that the universities were not really universities then. They were seminaries. So you need a time when universities are not seminaries, when they are expanding, when there are dangers that seem analogous or faintly analogous to what happened before. In other words, what we lack really is a good history of scholarship. Criticism and interpretation are part of scholarship. They are a complex. The history of criticism is not good enough in itself. It can be justified, but you must have a history of interpretation as well as a history of criticism, and a history of scholarship, of course not scholarship narrowly conceived. Someone like Edward Said in his book *Orientalism*, whatever quarrels one may have with matters of opinion, opens that area of understanding how scholarship is often ideologically oriented.

There has been an attempt by Robert Weimann to see the New Criticism as ideologically motivated, but it's far too crude a study.

What of The Dialectical Imagination *by Martin Jay? Of course none of the intellectuals he deals with are American.*

You go too fast. Let me double back a minute. You can take any of the great English poets. You can take Spenser and you can determine how, during the eighteenth century with the Spenserian revival, the question of unity raises itself or is challenged through the presence of Spenser. The emphasis on unity had excluded too much. So the new poetics, suggested by the reimportation into the national consciousness of Spenser, centers not on unity of action but on unity of design. You don't give up unity, but you realize that something is wrong. Spenser can't be unified in the same way as certain other poets.

In the case of Milton there was trouble all the time, but it surfaced as the Satanic heresy with Blake's and to some extent Shelley's feeling that the real hero of *Paradise Lost* was Satan, which splits that poem in a schizophrenic manner. Even now, there is a lot of power to this suggestion. The portrait of Satan is so strong that whatever the teleology of the poem, from the point of view of poetry rather than divinity much can be said for the greatness of poetry when Satan is there—although I have argued against the Satanist position. I have argued that the real hero of *Paradise Lost* is the creation, and I argue that not from any ideological principle, but because Book Seven contains some of Milton's greatest poetry.

So in each case you could find that an author is prematurely unified or given too early a resting place, a requiem, in criticism.

Wasn't Shakespeare the most obnoxious to his early critics because of a "lack of unity"? The first reaction critically was that he was "primitive"; secondarily there was the simplistic reaction of the je ne sais quoi, or merely the inexplicable; yet, the preserve of "reason" is still maintained.

Generally critics can make an exception for Shakespeare, as Dr. Johnson does, through a restricted genius theory. Once the Romantics come along, particularly the German Romantics, there is no restricted genius theory. Restricted genius is called talent, but genius by its definition is unrestricted and cannot be defined. This throws real art to genius. Then a question of limits, *Endlichkeit* or *Unendlichkeit,* or how to bound the infinite arises, and that's part of the aesthetic problem which the Romantics raise.

It's quite right to cite Shakespeare, because with some potent exceptions, there have been no incisive studies of him. Now the general level of Shakespeare scholarship is quite high, strangely enough, but there is very little that you would really single out. Shakespeare infects the writers; he pushes them to a competent level of thinking.

At the same time, he is a phenomenon of such scope, so "myriad minded," as Coleridge says, that it is indeed hard to reduce him or to conform him to one mind.

What has been the reaction of Marxist critics to your work?

Muscular Marxism is not happy with my work for several reasons. I am part of the late late show in advanced bourgeois capitalism. I still insist on the mediation of literature and of academic institutions. I have no urge to get to a radically new structure that would be beyond literature. I do occasionally lose my patience with the academy, even if it is changing and becoming less isolationist, at least in America.

There are unfortunate aspects to that isolation, due to the economic and market pressures that reach right into the curriculum. The professors seem to have less autonomy now than they possessed, *when* they did possess it. Even in private universities, the processes of budget making tend to be centered now in the administration, in something equivalent to the provost's office. So communication between what is often called the "central administration" and faculty is less fluid, less creative presently than before.

Marxist critics of literature say that they are writing about works of art. They're not?

They are writing about culture. It depends on what Marxism you go to. There is a genuine Marxist question as to what sort of work a literateur does; that's a metaphor, "work," but it's an honest metaphor, and it should induce thought, whether one is a Marxist or not. The naive Marxist may feel that there's a possibility of unalienated labor, and that, in its ideal form, literature projects the concept of unalienated labor. In any case, when we talk about the work of art, or as I like to say, about the work of reading, we still need some explanation what the word *work*, as in "work of art," really means. Competent Marxist thought would approach this through the notion of praxis and how reading Sartre's and other essential texts on praxis open up our limited notion of "practical criticism."

Obviously, I don't want to lose the independence of the classroom. The communal work of interpretation that goes on there is crucial. But that is no reason to evade larger social or cultural questions which often fall under the category of praxis.

Sartre himself never became a member of the Communist Party. Do you think he mistrusted the formula of organized Marxism?

I can only speak for myself. I don't know what my group is, what my political adhesion is. However, I would find it difficult to belong to a formal political group. In America, there's no problem at present. One is a registered Democrat or Republican, and there is usually a certain interchangeability, or at most a local or regional difference. If that were true of Marxism or socialism, if there were this kind of decentralization or tolerance of difference within nations or regions, then perhaps there would be no problem with affiliation. Where the doctrine or the apparatus is more centralized, then there is a problem. Someone like myself could belong to a party with a firm political doctrine—if he were free to try to find his own changes in that doctrine.

Has political and critical language become so conventional that the only antithesis is "Marxism"? In other words, why has Marxism so strongly become the means of antithetical discussion, too obviously the supposed alternative to middle-class political thought and conventional criticism?

I don't think Marxism is "antithetical" in Europe. It may seem antithetical in America because of our distrust of doctrine, religion and strong types of conceptualization in politics—but that goes not only for Marxism or the Left. It also goes for doctrines of the Right. Yet, even if the Moral Majority and members of the extreme Right wing are in some places feared, there is no sign that they are as feared as movements of the political left.

I know the intellectual scene in France better than in Germany or Italy—though I do know it a little in Germany, where there is a long history of genuine engagement with German philosophy itself which never quite frees itself from Hegel. Marxism also never cuts itself off from Hegel. But in France you have, in the 1930s, a reception of Husserl and Heidegger, and in France you also have certain central figures, like Sartre, who tie a knot, who are not just "university professors," but—in Sartre's case—an intellectual and a philosophical writer who expresses himself also in stories, novels, dramas, while engaged in political action. So there is an interpenetration of activities.

One might claim that Sartre's literary works are not Marxist. Nevertheless, they are impregnated with Marxist concepts and philosophical ideas translated into the shape of persons. Somehow the abstract concept has become concretized. In bad form, this may turn into caricature or allegory, but at least a tradition of such active political writing or fiction exists. So it is hard to neglect it.

Another thing to be remarked is: why cannot writers in America represent intellectuals without caricaturing them? Why is it that there was so much scandal about *Mr. Sammler's Planet?* Most of the time you get academic novels in which the professor's love life is central, or where the interest in students always turns on sex. There is a patent dishonesty or "bad faith" whenever intellectual conversation takes place, so that the entire intellectual life, as represented in these novels, is a parody.

American intellectuals have to decide whether the German and French traditions, including Marxism, mean enough *for them* so that they should be studied carefully. Vulgar Marxism or vulgar deconstructionalism is no better than vulgar Freudianism. Can there be a "cultural translation" of Hegel? Is there a way of taking Derrida out of his own text-milieu into an English and American text-milieu? Isn't this the kind of thought-experiment intellectuals are supposed to attempt?

What are the manifestations of political interest on college campuses now?

Politics on the part of students is totally justified, but takes the wrong channels, of unhistorical, deracinated conceptualization.

You refer to the basic techniques, those of pressure groups and electioneering? Imitations of the "heroic"?

Yes. Pure contemporaneity, the kind of demotic or slang exchange of concepts like *alienation, class warfare, exploitation,* and so on. Whereas there would be a closer alliance between history and literature if our own students read such things as accounts of state trials or pamphlets of the periods, not because there is any claim of direct influence on literature, but because just *this* too is part of literature; that is, literature in the larger sense. This is part of what would have been a natural component of their minds, just as newspapers are in our minds. It would ground the political interest of students and give it a general historical backing. It shouldn't take away from any present-day political activism, but it would make it more reflective.

Wouldn't part of that reflection be to recognize the cyclical nature of change and stability, or even terror and repression, in the loss of order?

Take the fear of the loss of order. Even if one has not been mugged, all one has to do is go to a modern movie in which there might be an episode of a motorcycle gang isolating a motorist and then violating him or her. This arouses terrifying feelings.

If one thinks of a society in which this may have been common or at least as common as in our society, where there were only certain safe areas, enclaves beyond which nothing seemed safe, perhaps there could be more understanding about the means of order, why the concept of order pertained with such pathos, such persistence. It's still here, "law and order."

We don't transfer it to literature, because literature is the one place where the difficulties of that concept could be tested. Rather than using literature as a means of order, we now seem to be using it as a place where order becomes questionable in a cathartic or testing fashion. But I doubt that this was there before. Whatever the inner disorder of *Paradise Lost* it was a statement of order, a vision of order. I'm not so sure about Blake's poetry, but I can be sure that it was so in Milton.

Blake does have an incessantly geometrical placing of opposites, however.

He probably saw more deeply the adversary relation, how too much order breeds disorder. But to go into this, one would have to insist that students of literature have some knowledge of legal principles, of jurisprudence, conceptually or through the reading of things that were transcripts of trials or even pamphlets that might have circulated and affected the consciousness of the artists of that time, including a thorough reading of Marx and other political theorists.

The issue of the balance of power?

The principle of the balance of power, or natural law as against positive law, of the relation of labor to economic value—one of our troubles is that we have completely separated the study of law and the study of literature, the study of economics and the study of literature.

Do you see that there is a compatible organic principle in the accumulation of changing, written custom in literature, criticism, and the common law?

Compatible—do you mean some kind of overall view?

That there may be organic relations—

Organic with each other—I don't know if I would use the term *organic*. No, I wouldn't use that. We don't know enough to have supervisory concepts here. I would say that there would be correlations, but the character of those correlations is still to be found out, and I would also want to analyze the very concept of organic, why we use organic in order to point to a certain kind of coherence.

Well, the term "organic" was itself a revolutionary metaphor in the sense of generating new life. The idea of generation is powerful in Shelley, for instance. Why should it have been so powerful an idea

for the Romantics when its origin is agricultural, which is so con-
servative because it is so cyclical? How did the romantics break that
metaphor loose from its setting?

Agricultural experience can be conservative, but if you take it one stage further, take the botanical metaphor, at least, one step further, as in Derrida, and talk about dissemination in its punning senses, then, of course, it is not so conservative.

Is that organic metaphor?

It is fascinating what Derrida does with botanical terms, with flowers of speech.

But let's go back before discussing Derrida to a matter mentioned
earlier, that of discourse in the academy, the matter of decorum.
This itself has its own cycle. There are obvious cycles of style that
accompany and precede Brooks, T. S. Eliot's criticism, Arnold, and
before that, a decorum that eventually refers to Addison and Dryden.
Now, if one picks up an academic journal of any kind, there is a
decorum that is patently out of this tradition. Now what do you
mean by "decorum," that the "decorum" in Europe is different?
Do you mean that the place of the writer is slightly more elevated
and, in Europe, includes critics?

Leaving aside what decorum is generically, one way in which it can be breached for many Anglo-American readers is by a critic allowing himself liberties of style or *allowing himself a style,* in fact, rather than making, like a dog, gestures of submission, tail wagging before the work of art, or "obeying" the voice of the master whom it does not understand, by putting its head down, and so on.

There are so many examples of this, but one might be Una Ellis-
Fermor's essay on Shakespeare's Troilus and Cressida *which follows*
these rules of critical language, and the literary art becomes a kind
of "calling," and criticism celebrates a "communion." The words
are "work of art," "elevation," so that one is raised through a chaos
of a play to a kind of contrived hypostatic union. However, the
criticism is in abeyance. Would this be an example?

It depends on how you conceive of the function of criticism.

Before going into that, let me say that this kind of essay can be very intelligent. I mean not intelligent *vis à vis* the work of art but an intelligent use of the proposition that criticism is clearly subordinate to a secondary function or is an aid in the analysis of literature. A novelist, although I think he started as a critic, had a debate with me that was recently published in *Novel*. He also objects to that; he doesn't like hermeneutic critics, as he calls them, who inflate themselves in the sense that they don't tell us much about the form of the work of art, who, by always talking about the human condition or existential matters, or by dealing with concepts, don't really inform us about the work of art. This shows a certain *malaise*, he believes.

Now it is true that this may be a break in the decorum of criticism. Criticism has been imprisoned in the same style for many years now, especially in Anglo-America. Some have broken out of that style, but they have been writers of fiction. Lawrence can get away with a great deal in his comments on American authors, but others can't. Now if I wrote a novel or two, because then I would be a novelist, readers might accept an unusual style in my criticism.

Denis Donoghue mentioned in a review of Irving Howe that "writer" in Europe is inclusive of "critic" and "novelist" and other genres. Is that the different "decorum" of writing in Europe you are talking about?

That's what I'm talking about in the Barthes' piece. Sure, the change has now occurred via France twice: first, I think, although my history may be shaky, in the eighteenth century with Voltaire. He conceived his fundamental social role to be that of a writer, not a gentleman, as when he went to Congreve who didn't want to be visited as a "writer," who wanted to be visited as a "gentleman." Voltaire said something like "There are enough gentlemen in France: it is the writer I want to meet." Voltaire saw himself as a writer. The tremendous intellectual energy which led to the Encyclopedists and everything else in France—that explosion of writing and knowledge—was part of an energy that became revolutionary.

Now there was a great deal of explosive writing in England, but much of it was from Grub Street and much of it was really subordinated to party purposes.

Anyway, that tradition of the writer or man of letters . . .

Well, such writing is never anthologized either . . .

You mean in the eighteenth century?

And later.

It isn't really except through the satires. Only highly specialized scholars get interested in such ideas.

But the man of letters is established, if I'm not mistaken, in eighteenth-century France and is a counter-social concept: that is, the writer transcends his birth as defined by social status or class. It is that which moves to the fore in questions of *écriture* where the basic energy, the basic thing, is writing. Whether you are doing fiction, poetry, sociology—whatever—you are a writer. Irving Howe, a sharp and relentless critic, shows you don't have to be European to be a significant man of letters. I find Howe more exact in his analysis of the text itself than Edmund Wilson—though *Axel's Castle* remains a classic.

There is some correspondence with the concept of "intellectual," of course. What is now called *écrivain* was then called *intellectual.*

Part of the problem in the 1930s because of the influence of Marxist questioning, was "What kind of *work* does the intellectual perform?" Does the intellectual really do work, or how can we define his work?

Another recurrence. That's vulgarly "Puritanical."

Yes. Are intellectuals engineers of the soul? We are doing it now in the academy. The capitalist version of that is to ask about the "productivity" of teachers. That is no less egregious than the other question, and shows from the capitalist side how we are beginning to ask the same questions with the same crude and disastrous effect. The raising of the question is interesting, but the attempt to methodize answers in terms of specific *ergons* of work is a disaster.

Let me ask you, then, about some of the ruses of the American academy. There is a standard of productivity, particularly at publicly financed institutions. Also there is an absence of intellectual tradition, if not place, contrary to a European scene for the use of the intellect, and, beyond that, little nationalistic pride in art itself. So Americans have tried to paper this over with some national funds, grant money, but even in the academy, where does the intellectual stand? He doesn't seem to have any place to stand, so what does he do? Does he then try to become a person with a certain kind of form, with a certain manner or even mannerisms? Is the academy itself often no more than a mannerism?

We've lost the prestige of the scholar who spent much of his time developing and evangelizing concepts of order of the English eighteenth century, and we have lost to some extent even the evangelical prestige contrary to that, of the Romanticists, because even so much historical backgrounding seems difficult.

The profession has entered an era of mass education. What we are confronting are the problems of that important experiment. What it involves has only recently come home to us, and I can't say much about it because we are in the midst of an evolving situation. I can say something general regarding the place of the intellectual, or whether he will have a place. Obviously he has to do two things at once. He has to insist, almost as an article of faith, that he has as much of a right to teach and to exist and to make a good living as the businessman has, and priorities which threaten that are to be fought. But then he must know how to fight politically.

You see, one new element that recently entered is that we don't know how long private universities can survive. They are ectypal. There are very few of them, very few distinguished private universities. They have come to rely more and more on government funding which they resisted for a long time. But government funding, as we all know, draws with it certain obligations and inspection procedures. The "family" of alumni feels less and less in control. As they feel less and less in control they give less and less. Where will this end?

As in all businesses, the cost of meeting federal standards of control is also something to be considered. I say this is a new element because if private universities should cease to be except in name, and if the state universities which have always been dependent on legislatures are kept even more dependent than the private institutions, then freedom of inquiry as we know it, though it may exist in name and be guaranteed by certain rules and laws, may not really exist because everybody will be doing a very low order of academic work. The initiative will have passed from the teacher and the tradition in which the teacher worked to the consumer and the client who himself may be manipulated by external interests. So, a very delicate balance of forces will have been destroyed.

That's one danger I foresee without a remedy in mind, except to urge that some of us in the profession become more statesmanlike, more political. Joining a union or AAUP, though it may help locally, will not be enough to improve the larger picture.

What to do about universal education, mass education? We are still learning. One thing we have learned is that while we have the skills to produce literacy we are not doing it too well, because the nontraditional student for whom we have developed the skills doesn't seem to be motivated. So the question is why he or she is not motivated. It may be that we have underestimated the pain, the sheer pain, of having to learn reading and writing. We may have underestimated it because the previous generations suffering from illiteracy came from homes in which there was nevertheless a respect for writing and reading. That's particularly true of Jewish kids from very poor classes who were illiterate not because they were from illiterate families but because they had to start again, and often had to hold a job in order to do anything. In that sense they were from the poorest strata.

But the problem with many students now coming in is that they are from a culture that is primarily oral. What is to be done with students from this culture?

It may be more difficult than we thought to switch from oral to written. Such a student may feel that the acquisition of written skills is repressive. Other cultures have felt that. Therefore it has to be made clear, deeply clear, that writing is not repressive. At least a balance must be recognized: can written skills fertilize, can they fructify an oral culture, or do they always mean giving up a great deal, the imposition of alien strata? I think that's what we're learning.

One can be reminded of many poems; one, particularly, talks about the disjunction of magic and literacy: "Theirs was the giant race before the flood."

What does Richard Hurd say, almost a century later? We have lost the world of fine fabling.

Actually, it passed into a mimetic mode, the novel, and so emerged again. I think that's the pattern, and it is one thing literary history does teach that we are not transmitting.

By the immense prejudice in favor of technology and the technological way of teaching, all emphasis has fallen on artificial ways of teaching literacy and stimulating motivation with little follow–up. Now one could really make a convincing case that generations have always moved this way, that is in terms of literary history, from an art form which was purely potential, even low life, or considered as such. I'm not saying the forms necessarily originated from the folk. They may have been what was called *gesunkenes Kulturgut,* part of a higher culture that had somehow filtered down or found its way into popular culture. But this does not alter the fact that the oral and the popular, like the ballad, at some point became quite elaborate, complex, sophisticated.

In general, what we call literature has moved that way. It has moved either from this previous, lower state, or it has integrated itself with existing high literature in some way. There always were such tensions, fights and battles. So I don't think, I can't believe, that we are in a totally new situation.

You have often mentioned the plight of the humanities and asked what could be done to help them out of their barrios. *Do you have anything more you would like to say about the subject?*

One would like to know why the profession that has more to do with the life and death of literacy in this country is economically depressed. Certainly there's always been a streak of anti-intellectualism in this country. This, however, has been complicated by the profession's own anti-intellectualism. Aside from this problem, however, I think that we have in a peculiar sense isolated ourselves; I refer to departments of English, the field of English, though it goes for the other humanities too. We have arranged things so that the brightest, the best students only would be admitted. Yet of those admitted the brightest and best would go back into the academy.

This meant that only the "dropouts" went into the public walks of life, or those that proved to be unmotivated by the humanities. But where does that leave us? It leaves us with no representation outside the academy. We have no one talking for us out there. This is an impossible situation and we are reaping its fruits. Until we find a way to get our best and brightest students into public walks of life, not as a second best but as a first choice, so that those out there are either motivated by the humanities or are not in public life or business because they have dropped out of the humanities, or because of not getting a job in the academy, we in the humanities are always going to be in a depressed state.

I don't see any solution unless we find a way to motivate our students to seriously consider public service. I don't mean that the academy is *not* public service. Of course it is public service. But going into business, into legislation, law, economics, and so on—I don't know why our students are not doing it except that they have an idealized view of academic life. If we could only disabuse them a little and say that the academy is just like any other business at some level, that there is just as much pettiness, just as much competition and so on.

I don't know how to demystify the academy because obviously I don't want the demystification to be absolute. Those in the profession know that the academy does protect its members, but it is by no means a free and easy, genteel place.

What may impress your readers is the absence of easily recognizable "schools" of criticism; that is, while there is a reading of Freud and others in your interpretations, there is no use of your sources as a critical recipe. What is striking about a lot of criticism is the use of sources as prescriptions, the use of Aristotle by the Chicago school, the use of Freud in a primitive matching of patterns and vocabulary, the use of Marx in simplified "Marxist" criticism. How does the critic avoid the constraints of such patterns?

I'm reminded of someone who complained in a review of one of my books that I never stand still enough on the page for him to catch the meaning. That is the other side of the diversity.

Well, it is interesting that you bring a Eu opean background to your criticism, that you use Freud, for instan e, and through him, explicate Derrida and language as a "code."

I suppose that having had an interest in comparative literature is part of it, but that has its own dangers because there is a type of comparative literature characterized by influence study which is intensely, minutely historical. Incidentally, I enjoy reading it because it leaves my mind free of supervening interpolations. Interpretation is interpolative as well as comparative. The older kind of comparative study, in its antiquarian cast, is necessary, but since all disciplines change, comparative literature also cannot stand still.

To come back to your question: I don't see an intrinsic reason why a more philosophical type of literary criticism couldn't have developed in America. Perhaps Freud became "Freudianism" too quickly; perhaps monolingualism prevented real contact with speculative thinkers in the hermeneutic and post–Hegelian mode. I still remember discovering Sartre's essays collected in *Situations I*, the powerful way they linked fictional technique to philosophical and metaphysical issues. In Kenneth Burke, especially, a comparably speculative vigor was apparent: *Attitudes toward History,* for example, has exemplary insights of the Sartrean kind, though Sartre pursued them in a more focused and relentless way, putting *responsibility* on the individual artist rather than diffusing it, like Burke, over the national, cultural scene. Another matter that made me sensitive to philosophy was its almost puritan approach towards language—I had known what propaganda could do, the "dictatorship of the propagandists" I mentioned in the little book on Malraux; and so I was determined to see literature as a critique of rhetoric though from within rather than from without, the outside view being the one often taken in philosophy from Plato on.

One thing a European background teaches is that the study of philosophy, of language, and of literature connects with one another. There may also be a personal and temperamental factor in my chameleon style of thought. It has to do with the sense I have of myself as a writer, and in my younger days I thought just of writing and teaching and never of a specified professional role. I like to write. I was very naive about these problems for a long time. Something in me later didn't just throw off the naiveté, but picked up the naiveté as an important moment of development. There was a kind of Hegelian sublation of the naive.

There are your critics who complain about terms such as "Hegelian sublation." What does that mean?

Yes. Well, by sublation—most of the time I usually translate the Hegelian term as *elation*—all it means, and I don't think it's a technical term worse than any other which we use and abuse—

Mimesis? Epode? Peripety?

Right. Through sublation we know that a past stage of thought or mode of being never quite disappears. According to Hegel there is an orderly interiorization of that earlier stage, and here one might use psychoanalytic rather than Hegelian categories. It's a question of incorporation or interiorization and how an earlier stage is still present in a later stage.

I don't know. There may be botanical and there may be physiological metaphors too.

But what I was saying is that I enjoy thinking, and I enjoy writing only because it puts pressure on me and on thinking. I don't enjoy writing as a product, as something that is merely an end product, a commodity.

In fact, I suppose I would prefer that thinking might exist in a circuit that would not have to eventuate in the frozen form of article or essay.

And it may be this attitude, which has been philosophical and literary both, that has kept me open and has prevented my thought from taking fixed forms.

On the other hand, I'm extremely interested in genres, in types, the way they support one's thinking in conventions. That has to be added.

What disconcerts many readers of criticism like mine is the combination of these two activities, the philosophical openness, the willingness to approach everything and to start all over again, and the intense interest in historically determined, or at least historically visible, genres and conventions. And I suppose that this combination doesn't always succeed in me, and those two lines may not even be consistent with each other.

Another autobiographical question: Your book on Wordsworth is
impressive for many reasons, one being its tone. How old were you
when you finished writing it?

I finished it in 1963, which means I was thirty-four.

What was the attraction to Wordsworth?

The attraction was very early. It started in England where I had
my secondary education, and it was instinctive. I lived in Bucking-
hamshire during the war. It was a very rural part of England, most
parts of England actually were. I was free and roaming. Even though
Wordsworth is not an intense nature describer and this was not the
Lake District but a very different landscape, Wordsworth's type of
meditation, a capacity for solitary thinking nature seemed to enable,
must have suited me at that point. It was not a thinking about
personal relations. It was a *minimal* thinking about relations with
other people. Though that entered, it entered only as a moment. It
was not a very consumer–oriented thinking. When one is in the
presence of nature as relatively open and mild as that of Bucks,
there's an appeal.

Then you know, in *The Unmediated Vision* the first poet I dealt
with was Wordsworth. I don't know why I went back. I was just
gradually drawn back to write something more sustained.

However, the paradox was that the book on Wordsworth had
an easier acceptance in America than in England because of, again,
the fixity of scholarship.

You wrote it in America, didn't you?

I wrote it in America, but in a sense it was based on my earlier,
more English experience. English scholarship had imprisoned
Wordsworth. My view is not all that unconventional—Wordsworth
as nature poet with a certain spiritualizing power is still there, but
English scholarship didn't recognize that I was talking about this. I
was using terms that had either been lost or were used only in an
impressionistic way. I imported, in auxiliary fashion, but quite deliberately, terms from other traditions, such as the *Akedah-apoca-*
lypse distinction or the question of individuation which came from
psychoanalysis on the one hand and from Hegelian thinking on the
other, and the whole emphasis on consciousness.

As soon as there is talk about consciousness, the stages of individual consciousness, and one draws each term into an analytic,
one goes totally against a kind of scholarly appreciation which insists that poetry, if it is a kind of thought, is very different from
philosophical, analytic thought.

*What was the relation of Heidegger and Freud to your book on
Wordsworth?*

It was much more Hegel. There was little Freud at that time. I
may have touched Heidegger, but I certainly didn't understand Heidegger at the time. I did understand Hegel. Some Freud. More Jung,
actually, than Freud.

You went from Hegel to Freud?

I don't see it that way. I don't feel that my interest in Freud
came in at a chronologically precise stage. So that's hard to answer.
My interest in Freud is through my interest in interpretative activity
and its history. One has only to dip into *The Interpretation of
Dreams,* which was always a central book for me, to see something
extraordinary in terms of the hermeneutic activity that is going on.
It had nothing to do with Freud's sexual theory, except insofar as I
felt that interpretative activity always dealt with something akin to
sublimation on the one hand and desublimation on the other. Freud's
understanding, whether it was ultimate or not, of the base—the
material, the physiological, or from whatever the mental-spiritual
interpretative activity started—I found extraordinarily powerful.
His ability to get from one to the other never ceased to amaze me.

*Isn't it becoming more apparent that Freud's own interpretations
make languages much less simple and less univocal?*

Again, there are certain easy correlations between that and
modern views in poetics on ambiguity and connotation. I feel that
the concept of ambiguity has to be reconceived through Freud and
made more radical. It may have to be more radical than Freud himself
conceived it, and that is why Derrida is important. Not that one can
live on ambiguity or any kind of radical procedure, but one must
pass through the fires of interpretation and the slipperiness of language. One does not therefore say immediately, "Look. Be careful.

There's ice. Hold on or change your shoes." But one understands the slipperiness is, to a large extent, constitutive.

That is what most attracted me in Derrida. My contact with his writing is relatively late. I probably had read no Derrida before about '68. My real interest in him did not come until *Glas* appeared, and that was 1974. Before that I had read in him but had not particularly studied any essay.

For those who haven't seen the text of Glas, *what is it like? Is it a printed Rosetta Stone? It's a different book, isn't it?*

It is. It's a fun book, and, as you know, is divided into two columns and juggles two commentaries at the same time, one on Hegel and one on the French convict-turned-writer, Genet. Those two columns often become three columns and there is a lot of typographical spacing within them. Like any book, it may be read vertically, but at the same time one can glance from column to column and find remarkable correspondences.

It is a philosophical work of art.

I said previously that one reason English tradition found it difficult to accept the book on Wordsworth is that it had its own notion of the kind of thinking, or nonthinking, that poetry is. I am in great sympathy if that tradition had really analyzed the notion of nonthinking and had understood that language is a form of nonthinking, but it left that aside.

From Wordsworth to Derrida—what a jump! Derrida would be ridiculous to insist on their affinity, but a certain aspiration, a certain intuition had surfaced, not only in Hegel, but during the romantic period in the Schlegels, in the poetics and aesthetics of the Schlegels, more than in English romanticism. English romanticism more instinctively, perhaps, without having a theory for it, also pursued an understanding that art, as Coleridge said, has its own logic. Yet as soon as you use the word logic, you are lost, because you are accused of false analogy.

So when I say that Derrida's *Glas* is a philosophical work of art, I mean it is a rebirth of philosophy out of the spirit of art.

As opposed to historical chronology, generally conceived cause and effect?

Oh yes, certainly that doesn't enter. But in the modern period there is this antithesis of philosophical thinking and artistic thinking, or style and thought, as if thought at best had no style, as if that was to be purged from thought.

Now we can put this many ways. One simplified way in which Derrida has been understood and lets himself be understood on occasion, is that even philosophy cannot avoid metaphor. Philosophy can never reduce its language to univocal terms, but I think that's the least interesting way of putting it.

What does Derrida himself say about style?

Well, it's a lively term and Derrida in *Glas* is very good on that. He points out that style, etymologically, can also be a floral term. He plays elaborately. But there's also a lot that's *inky* in Derrida— that's ink-horn. He loves dictionaries. *Glas* in a sense . . .

Is glossary?

There's glossary.

Glass? Mirrors?

There is the sense of prefixes, etymology, play. He has his own pedantic erudition, but it really is transcended in a marvelous kind of playfulness.

Glas, though, if one speculates on its form—I suppose the fact that it's in two columns evokes dictionaries. Some have said that it reminds them of the *Talmud,* and that's possible too. But Derrida's debt to the great dictionary makers, especially to Littré and Wartburg is enormous.

Now obviously he couldn't have made use of that form of stored knowledge which Littré and Wartburg represent without an animus, without a driving conception, but dictionaries and nomenclatures are essential to feed his thought.

Does he play off the seeming absoluteness of dictionary definitions against themselves? Isn't that part of the book?

He shows there is no such absoluteness. Yet Littré retained an idea of correctness. That is, if the first modern dictionary is the dictionary of the French Academy, it certainly was undertaken to fix the language and to purify it. Littré maintains that ideal by thinking that certain words have a pathological development, that they shouldn't have gone in this or that direction.

But, in fact, Derrida shows how slippery etymologies and meanings are.

The Wartburg dictionary is mind-boggling when you see cognates and the most amazing slidings and slippings, the *Bedeutung-swandlung.*

Often oral and not written? Spoken transliterations?

That's right. It's probably because they were oral but also because there may have been mistakes or because spelling wasn't fixed.

It's a fascinating jungle that you enter into.

Doesn't art often have its own kind of suspicious dialectic that anticipates later comment? James Joyce's story "Clay" is a pun on clé, the Gaelic word, meaning left; the main character of the story, Maria, is presented in a sinister fashion and in fact, constantly moves toward the left, turns left, in her travels in Dublin. Of course, the story is also filled with sexual references of all kinds, and the French word clef, pronounced like the title of the story, means "key." Now, while the story may be read in several simplified ways, it undoubtedly, and by design, traverses the normal limits of language in a very dynamic way. Is this partly what Derrida is about?

It's a good point. One of the seeming scandals is that Derrida imported this into philosophical discourse. What he was doing had been done before, in art. It shows how deeply the neoclassical concept of the separation of genres is still with us.

It lessens the appeal of literature for the other humanities, doesn't it?

It may. I'm not sure the other humanities are in better shape though, and I don't think the whole burden rests on us. I don't know what the situation is, really, in history as a discipline. I doubt that it's very much better, although clearly there are more provinces in history and you are allowed to become an inhabitant of a historical province in a more thorough sense than we, whose main burden seems to be more and more the teaching of elementary standard English.

I would like to ask about the last part of your essay on Derrida in the book you edited for the English Institute, Psychoanalysis and the Question of the Text. *You conclude it with a tribute to Walter Benjamin. How much do you identify with him?*

I think it would be of value to look more closely at displacements, of the way that the migration of ideas and even the course of literature are influenced by political persecution, and by people having to displace themselves from one culture to another.

I don't mean to say that if you stay at home you can't be a writer. Benjamin, in fact, tried to stay at home. Writing as such posed for him the problem of the form that truth takes; whether it can be transmitted as truth or whether writing does not dilute or distort it, writing being exilic in essence. An antinomy arises between truth and transmissability, similar to Kafka's sense of the precariousness of tradition or spiritual inheritance. How can one be creative within that situation? How can one prevent oneself from becoming a "destructive character" who liquidates tradition even further by the claim he is transmitting it, that is, making it available? Benjamin's style of writing conserves that problematic as well as attempting to save some household gods from persecution.

There's an ironic strength arising from persecution?

Yes. This has many facets, as is indicated by Leo Strauss's book, *Persecution and the Art of Writing.* Maybe there's always persecution even in one's own native country, or there's always something, if you think of Freudian concerns, that is persecutory. If one doesn't have a persecutor one raises him up from within oneself, creating a movement of self-alienation. The writer is a refugee who finds a home in his writings.

Erich Auerbach wrote an essay in which he tried to actually pinpoint the idea of the writer as a person without a country or as someone who had no abiding nationality.

However, I would modify this by saying that the concept of nationality has itself been overhomogenized, like the notion of unity. And when we talk of English literature, well, is Joyce part of English literature or is he world literature?

But, no doubt, at this point in that particular essay there is an identification of myself with Benjamin.

Is Benjamin's condition, tragic as it was, not also a comment on the condition of being a scholar? Is not the scholar's activity in itself alienating?

I wouldn't use the term "alienating." Such words are always comparative. Being a scholar in America is no more alienating than being a scholar in Europe. In America, there is more mobility, more economic support. Although that is fickle. Unfortunately, many of our younger scholars have become "part-timers," wandering from position to position. If that continues, they won't contribute anything lasting to the academy or to American culture. They will just be babysitters for the eighteen to twenty-two year olds.

Alienation is a very specific concept in Hegel and Marx. I don't think we have a more than superficial or *ad hoc* analysis of intellectuals in America. I haven't gathered my thoughts completely, but what can be said is that in the 1930s and '40s, America was enriched by *émigré* scholars who had a considerable influence, not only on the humanities but on American life itself. This is continuing, but less dramatically. It seems to me unfortunate that the Frankfurt school, Theodor Adorno, Max Horkheimer, Herbert Marcuse, was only partially received in America after the war. Of a person like Leo Lowenthal, we knew only a few books and essays in English. American interest moves in waves, and we did have a Marcuse wave. He is still a significant intellectual personality who, having been caught up in 1960s politics, lost credit in some quarters. Yet if you read his *Eros and Civilization,* or his *One-Dimensional Man,* these are powerful tracts. I'm not sure that anyone else writing at that time in America is that forceful and culturally prepotent. Neither book provides a close study of academic texts, then the mode, so the influence was more on the activists in the academy.

But one may ask another question. Is the intellectual an integral part of American society? Certainly not.

Are intellectuals an integral part of any *society?*

We do have the term "intelligentsia," and I can reflect on that. In America, there is a separation of church and state. This has also worked out to include a *de facto* separation between *literature* and *state*. I know that it sounds strange comparing literature to an institution like the church. But in Europe there was a model of the *littérateur*, the *homme de lettres*, which included political action or being allied with social forces and appealing to a large audience.

Particularly in France. Whatever one thinks of Mitterand, he is in fact a published author.

Yes. There is also the example of *Apostrophe*, which has no equivalent here. In France, intellectuals vie to get on this TV program which invites new or well-known writers or artists to talk and has an audience of several millions.

Recently during the turmoil over Bitburg, a German newspaper, which does not have a separate book review but integrates a feuilleton in its issues, published an essay, a very difficult essay, by Jürgen Habermas, under the title, "Defusing the Past: A Cultural and Political Tract."

So "culture politics" are simply a reality, for good or bad, in Europe. In America they don't exist, unless you follow the line of neo-Marxists such as Fredric Jameson in *The Political Unconscious*, for whom every cultural statement, every cultural manifestation has a political base. And journals like *Commentary* or *The New Criterion* try hard, like *Partisan Review* once did, to animate cultural quarrels. But to our common perception, culture does not play a political role, except in elementary educational areas in such issues as bilingualism. One may talk about the politics of culture but to substantiate it at the level of policy in governmental circles—that would be very difficult. In Europe, however, as everyone knows, there is a relation. As you said, Mitterand writes poetry. Claudel was a literary figure. So they do not separate the cultural and the political realms. In France there is a *Minister of Culture*. This is not window dressing. It must have some general influence even if you argue that it is overridden by the political. It is part of the public function and becomes a force to be reckoned with. One cannot pretend it is not there.

There's a famous story about Stalin calling up a favorite writer in the middle of the night and asking, "Do you think Mayakovsky is really a great poet?" The reason he asked was that Mayakovsky had written a poem circulating in Russia at the time which clearly satirized Stalin, a kind of allegory which didn't mention Stalin by name but made him apprehensive. He simply couldn't overlook the phenomenon and say, "Those snobbish *literati*."

The only example I can think of in the United States is the movement during the Vietnam War and the group that refused to attend Lyndon Johnson's "culture day."

When a President gives one day a year to culture, you can make a statement by abstaining!

I have two stories about André Malraux, the minister of culture under de Gaulle. Why, he was asked, did he have such an admiration for American writers? Malraux had written on Faulkner, and he thought the American novel was extremely important. He answered that the American writer needs just two things: a desk and a bottle.

The French writers (this is my addition) are always linked to vast metaphysical, political, who knows what, considerations. The American writer—it's not that he is necessarily alienated from his culture—but he sits down and concentrates, perhaps with his bottle of whiskey. The rest takes care of itself, at least from Malraux's point of view.

Having written a book on Malraux, I once wished to translate and edit a book of his essays. I was given his phone number, I called, the secretary answered. I said I wanted to speak with Malraux. She said, "Exactly whom do you want to speak to, Monsieur le Ministre or Monsieur l'écrivain?"

Now this sort of reply would be impossible in America.

Earl Butz?

Yes. Calling someone in the Cabinet to ask for Mr. Secretary or Mr. Author! In fact, with Malraux *écrivain* and *ministre* went together, and at that point had to be distinguished, however artificially. It is a characteristic of America, especially contemporary America, to keep these matters separate as in the nineteenth century. With Jefferson the French tradition still prevailed. But Henry James in the next generation said there was no milieu for an *American* writer. I haven't enough of an overall view to say whether this condition is good or bad.

One may talk about alienation, and implies by that term that academicians and writers are not deeply involved in the public sphere. I am not at all sure that such detachment or apparent detachment can be called "alienation." I do regret that writers cannot project their ethos into whatever community in America has the most say about policy. I've talked about the "executive thinking" of that community—"thinking," that is, without actual writing. Our experience, as people engaged in literature and the arts, especially in the verbal arts, is that you don't, you can't really *think* without writing. So one could certainly say that there are too many who have political influence on our lives and do not engage in the discipline of writing. They do not chasten or deepen their thoughts by writing. Therefore, they engage in "executive thinking," and leave the "writing" to others. That is a dangerous development. Everyone should do the kinds of thinking necessary to writing and policy making. "Ghostwriting" in governmental circles is, in this, a danger. I'm not naive enough to think that all politicians can write their own speeches, but it is quite obvious that Churchill wrote his own. It's also obvious that this adds power and persuasion. We just don't have that in America. To "overarticulate," to speak too well, is to put one out of the political arena. The example of Adlai Stevenson comes to mind.

But I haven't answered your question, which was preceded by a reference to Walter Benjamin. That is, what is the position of the Jewish intellectual?

Doesn't the Jewish intellectual have a double form of separateness?

Only double?

If there is an admitted isolation in this culture for those who deal with language and ideas, is there not also an extra isolation? Does American Jewish culture support the intellectual more than the native WASPs?

It cuts two ways. Some Jewish intellectuals redeem their natural isolation as writers by going back into the Jewish community which they then talk about and support and nourish. In that sense they do have a kind of arena. This has been more noticeable recently in response to a general return to ethnicity which has also affected Jewish intellectuals.

However, it can go the other way too. The Jews in America are still very much in a minority position. It's always been the fate of the Jews, though, that they have been perceived as being extremely influential, but in fact they have always been a minority with very limited influence. I have been studying this more because of charges, in the history of anti-Semitism, that Jews have controlled this and that, newspapers or centrally located financial institutions, for instance. All absolutely untrue. Hitler thought that the owner of *The Times* of London, Lord Northcliffe, was a Jew. He also identified Franklin Roosevelt as a Jew. It didn't matter if someone pointed out that Northcliffe or Roosevelt weren't Jews. Hitler would respond, "Well, they are under the Jewish influence!"

Today, of course, we know how little Roosevelt was under "Jewish influence"; he resisted Jewish migration to the United States during World War II. He also refused to divert any of the war efforts towards stopping the slaughter, the German extermination of the Jews. The myths in this area are enormous.

To return to our main subject. There are some who feel very vividly their minority status. In that sense there could be a feeling of alienation, but in America this has been noticeable only here and there. It hasn't been consistent. For instance, after the American entry into the First World War, there was a turning against German culture. So German Jews were faced with a double problem, even though they had been immigrants settled for a long time. Ludwig Lewisohn writes about this in his autobiography. He was a German Jew, and German culture was therefore part of him. There was no need to deny German culture just because the war had taken place accompanied by its fierce reaction. That period was very hard on Jewish intellectuals. For the first time they began to enter the academic mainstream. As they tried to enter, the opposition to them became quite visible.

You are referring to the exclusionary quotas in the United States?

There was a quota system for Jewish students attending the university, and more than a quota system, a blanket resistance, to hiring Jewish professors. Lewisohn was told that there was no chance for him to become a teacher at the university level.

We know also what happened to Lionel Trilling. Trilling was not a very visible Jew. He was Jewish and had some Jewish interests, but he tried very hard to be a part of English, even Anglophile, culture. But he encountered difficulties. Just how much we shall see when Diana Trilling finishes his biography. Still, something is known. Now this happened to someone who identified with English culture.

However, I think there was a change of sentiment because of the émigré professors of the 1940s and 1950s. They were recognized as significant scholars and eventually came to hold academic places. They weren't all Jewish—for instance, René Wellek. At any rate, Jews were allowed—I know that I am talking about a small segment here—to move into the academy. Yet at the time I came to Yale in 1955, there were only two or three Jewish professors in the humanities.

I would say that there existed at Yale until the 1960s what goes under the name of cultural anti-Semitism. There were no overt acts, but it makes no sense that there were no Jewish tenured professors of English or history unless Jews were thought "unfit" for those two disciplines of acculturation. With the 1960s there was a gradual movement of the Jewish intellectuals into the academy and tenure. Now would being accepted into the academy diminish the sense of isolation? I should think so. How it is when one looks into oneself is something else again. I would find it hard to insist that being a Jewish intellectual in America is a form of double alienation. I don't feel that. In honesty, one should propose another question: Is not the academic Jewish intellectual rather in danger of being alienated from the Jewish community, which is less intellectual than he is? In other words, it's not an extraordinary situation, since the Jewish intellectual has always felt alienated from the bourgeoisie. So the alienation would exist at that level whether one were a Jew or not. To some extent, it is important to overcome that. One could say that it is essential that the Jewish intellectual not enclose himself, as he now can, within the academy and forget about the community from which he sprang.

Read, for instance, Norman Podhoretz's *Making It*, which discusses and reveals the drive of the second generation, the children of the immigrants, to gain the culture and the language. Extraordinary. They did integrate themselves, but they became alienated from their parents. That's gone, or almost gone, within Jewish circles. So that now, strangely enough, the alienation is of the older type. The intellectual says to the community, "You don't know anything about history, about Jewish history. What are you going to do about it?" The burgher says, "Oh, I'm tired. I come home, I've been busy all day, I have children, I have family. I try to keep up so that my kids can get the best education." That kind of talk is a common and daily occurrence.

Yet I don't find any large scale alienation present, though structurally the humanities have unselfconsciously been based on classical and Christian culture. We study Spenser. In 1955 as a Jew, I taught my students Christianity by teaching them Spenser. This was necessary, for our literature comes from a culture that is basically Christian. Until the modern period, that is, between the Hebrew Bible and the modern American novel or Kafka, almost no Jewish classics are present in the curriculum. If you go into philosophy, you might read, if you're lucky, Maimonides.

For these reasons, I have pressed with others for the establishment of Judaic studies as part of the humanities, not as a separate entity, so that this tradition of learning which has been the most continuous in the West may achieve some sort of presence in the academy.

In that sense, there was alienation. Things as a Jew you had read you couldn't teach. They weren't shared. The Bible was out, the Hebrew Bible, partly because even though a private university doesn't have any restrictions on teaching, it was still difficult to bring the Hebrew Bible and its interpretive tradition into the curriculum. Insofar as it did enter the curriculum it was surrounded by a Christian interpretation. Even now if you discuss the Talmud people put on an indifferent or puzzled expression: they think of a strange, perplexing, esoteric document. It is a very difficult collection, certainly, but also an extremely important code that mixes law and legend. Even that form, where law and legend are not kept apart but presented side by side, should be studied. Here we are, at least as anthropologists, studying all kinds of distant cultures. However, one of the main religious cultures, the Jewish, did not really penetrate academic programs.

But now it has a chance. There is a true renascence in that area. So that was the alienation I felt. I was unable to bring my Jewish reading to teaching.

Do you see any chance that non–Jews will become involved in this curriculum?

I don't see why not. Why wouldn't a Christian . . .

Or humane atheist?

Or put it the other way: Why should a Christian or an atheist be all that interested in classical, that is, pagan, culture? If you see the Jewish learning tradition as being important in only a religious sense, well, of course, then its appeal is limited. However, if you have a kind of approach that humanists encourage and work with the historical imagination to open up difficult thinking other than what we are used to, the treasures of Jewish tradition are enormous—but different. The *idea of art* is not developed, for example. It's not that there is no art, but it is not as we understand Hellenic art, partly because there isn't as much plastic or pictorial work. The energy of the Jewish learning tradition goes mainly, though there are many exceptions even before the modern period, into writing, into legal thinking, into commentary but not into pictorialism, sculpture, music—of course we are talking chiefly about the premodern period.

So one has to approach this culture with a view that is not shaped by classical culture, or for that matter, Christian culture. If one gets involved in the classical work of art, in which the idea of the classical merges by the late eighteenth century into that of the autonomous work of art, then you would find it difficult to enter the Jewish learning tradition, which is text-dependent, nonautonomous. Yet, within that dependency the most extraordinary things happen—imaginative maneuvers, exegetical inventiveness, textual density. Of course, that is moot now, insofar as there is a secular Jewish art. Jewish writers obviously and without special difficulty are writing short stories, novels.

I have a special sympathy, however, with Cynthia Ozick's view that while the force of the Hebrew Bible is so great that every literature exposed to it "speaks Hebrew," Jewish writers are fundamentally at odds with the idea of art in gentile culture. Her debate, both loving and acrimonious, with Harold Bloom on the idolatrous, because iconolatrous, character of art simply affirms their common position that Diaspora Jews have not produced an art in the "Western" sense that is up to their achievements in other areas: science, law, commentary.

Let me qualify these comments about Jewish art and learning since Jewish writers have always borrowed from other cultures. They learned a great deal from Hellenism, for instance. They are not insulated. Think of the great Spanish era of poetry before the expulsion in 1492. The lyrical culture stimulated by Arabic poetics is enormous and exists both with and apart from the liturgical poetic tradition.

This exists in translation?

Jehuda Halévi is available but more should be available in translation. One might say that we don't know Arabic culture, either. So you are faced with an overcrowding of the curriculum, given the inquiring mind, even when that mind focuses on literature.

Is this material finding its way into Jewish studies?

A little bit. But your earliest question was whether non-Jewish students can participate? Yes. There are patterns they will recognize. The access is there, but what is one to gain by making the effort of entering the Jewish tradition? It could be argued that one always gains by the effort to understand another culture. But Jewish culture, though the most continuous in the West, has had little direct ramification in the way the classics have had after the Renaissance. European literature is dependent on the knowledge or the elaboration of the classics. However, we don't have a Hebrew renaissance in Western culture. There were stirrings of it in Europe when Hebrew began to revive as a modern idiom, but there is no canonical "intertextuality" as there is between Virgil and Milton or Milton and Wordsworth.

In the text-tradition of Judaism, you have a single if capacious book you have to enter: the Hebrew Bible. You then have to understand the relation of commentary to the Bible. A question is raised by this which fascinates me: Whether commentary is not always within literature, whether literature itself has not always been a development of commentary? One still has to define why literature is different from commentary on literature. But that question becomes more acute as you read within Jewish tradition characterized by the predominance of commentary which seems to move always within a magnetic circuit because it cannot rid itself of the spell of the Hebrew Bible. Every commentator knows the previous commentator, and has to make selections, or has to circumvent or subvert, but cannot neglect the antecedent. The postulate is that of continuation. There is then something within the Jewish tradition which is like the continuation of canonical classical sources in Christian Renaissance texts. Except there you have a transcultural movement, pagan to Christian, whereas in the Jewish tradition you have an inner modification. Everything claims to be an extension of Scripture.

What is the difference between criticism and commentary? You've written about criticism as a form of higher faculty or voice than many have wished to grant it.

I see commentary as a very large genre. I include scholarly books and not just line by line commentary or explication. I do grant commentary or criticism a "higher voice," as you put it, but that does not mean that I put it into a competitive relationship with literature. I try to break down the *a priori* evaluation of literature over essay and commentary. I don't see why we have to grant one a greater value than the other. It may be that much in what we call literature is more significant than commentary, and certainly commentary moves always within the field of force of literature. But this may be deceptive, as Lukács has said. Commentary may use literature for its own purposes. We may find, eventually, that we can more clearly see the symbiosis between literature and commentary.

What is remarkable about commentary is that it seems to be a field of weak forces. That is, it may be stronger than most grant it credit for being, but it represents itself as *dependent*. It is always a function for something that has preceded—a document, a previous commentary sometimes, often literature. That's how commentary represents itself, for whatever reason. I'm not sure what this gesture of obeisance means. On the other hand, many creative writers may go the other way and say: "To hell with the critics. I write my own stuff, and I don't care what they have to say." For this view, commentary is a card packed in chewing gum, something extra to market the primary product.

So each, text and commentary, is like a dialogue?

At best, like a dialogue. Now, the interesting thing about Derrida is that commentary comes into its own. Like Mallarmé's prose it takes unto itself the same intellectual complexity as poetry. Derrida's commentary on Hegel and Genet in *Glas* results in something more than commentary. It creates out of the commentary of a philosopher on literary and philosophical texts something very close to what we could call "art."

Isn't part of the confusion here the common literary anthology with its own debased "commentary," the overly literal and often factually inaccurate "notes" as the inevitably distended and distracting appendix? In some of the Hebrew texts, however, the commentary actually is a running and parallel printing next to the primary text.

Yes, also in the Talmud. Some texts are in larger type than others, but that simply means there is seniority or priority. However, there are still aspects of this to be explored. I don't fully understand, I must admit, what literature is when I read Kafka, where I am taken by the remarkable illusion which his novels impose on me. I am drawn into that world, and I can enter that world much more easily and lose myself in it more than in commentary. Commentary, by extruding another text, what it comments on, seems intrusive. We sense in it discontinuity, breaks, intellectual questions. It follows a line that interrupts itself or goes mazy on us.

So in your own mind this is still an unresolved perplexity?

Very unresolved! You cannot read commentary without a certain intellectual interest. Don't ask me to define intellect! You can read fiction, though, without being intellectual.

So your comments on criticism are in part intended for an academic audience which sees itself engaging in a debased idiom, "mere commentary"?

Well, perhaps I talk about this too much, but whatever peda-gogical function we accept and put on ourselves, we don't cease to be intellectuals.

So commentary should not stop with introductions and footnotes in anthologies?

Of course not, nor does it stop with an article in *PMLA*. I think the world of prose is what matters. The world of poetry matters too. I do not want to talk prescriptively. One would allow it to happen, let it happen, but it's not a prescription that one should be flighty in one's prose. But this is much too abstract, what I've been saying here. In Midrash (which simply means interpretations) the rabbis debate with each other. The debate is generally line by line, and was collected at some point in the medieval period. As they debate, you don't know why they go from one place to another, and you sometimes don't know on first perusal why they bring in other parts of Scripture. A mosaic is created. I feel occasionally that I really do see a structure there, a fascinating structure. So what I want to do is analyze the structure of that commentary. It always appends itself to a line or episode in Scripture, but the exact relation of that commentary, that rabbinical back-and-forth discussion of Scripture is not a pedagogical one, and it is not always an exegetical one. Other things are going on, and it is about these other things about which I would want to talk.

What do you mean by "other things"? Certainly your discussion will not be Aristotelian or syllogistic?

No. I can only say two things. There is a way in which many Midrashim allow themselves, under the guise of elaborating partic-ular lines of Scripture, to comment on subjects which, if not for-bidden, are holy. They evoke indirectly what you could call the divine life. The purpose of these commentaries insofar as they are not usable for Halakhah, whose main purpose is to clarify civil or ritual law, is just to talk about Scripture. You find them interested in what happens up in the heavens, or about the conversations Abra-ham may have had with God. They interpolate all kinds of things. It's an imaginative exercise which involves not only the human ac-tors, Jacob, Abraham, and so on, but human actors so close to God that they implicate God. Usually the writers do not speculate directly about God, but since Scripture is a reflection of not just the will but also the nature of God, that can be expressed in commentaries. And it gets to be fascinating. The rabbinical or what has come to be called the normative often stands side by side with mystical thoughts. Yet, the reader doesn't feel that they are mystical because their tenor is not Christian with a submission or overwhelming of the will. Instead, this commentary is always fading into another text. It never loses lines. It keeps moving *within* the bounding outline of the given text, however much it may look *through* those lines or reconstruct what is *between* those lines.

Aren't your comments "reverent" towards what is to be perceived as "sacred"? How is this then to be made more generally available? In other words, what I somewhat overhear in your remarks may be found also in certain pious interpretations of Christian authors, such as "Shakespeare the Roman Catholic," or the "Christianity of Milton," or the religious readings of Gerard Manley Hopkins—seminary or religious school readings, in other words—which include dogma but exclude criticism as such.

If so, it would not be in the spirit of the Jewish tradition, but of the Christian. "The spider love that transubstantiates all," as Donne phrases it. This principle of incorporative and somewhat vampirish or spidery charity is one of the glories of the Christian religion through the typological method. It exists much less in Jewish exegesis. There is the marvelous instance of the "Song of Songs." Yet the basic *biblia* which were put in the canon are very clearly writings that deal with God's relations to human society.

All I can see in your remarks are further expressions of the religious.

There is no document as old as the Hebrew Bible, which has so much criticism of the adventures or *Heilsgeschichte* of the people which are its subject. From the beginning, there was little piety in the Bible itself towards the people of God. If you wish, it is piety towards God, though I wouldn't call it that: fear, awe, but not *piety*. It's the wrong term.

What has made anti-Semites happy is that the Hebrew Bible itself gives them their ammunition. If the Bible hadn't given it to them, most Christian criticism of the Jews couldn't exist. The criticism is there within the Bible; hence there is tension between criticism and piety when we turn to the example of the Hebrew Bible itself. Internal adjustments and glossings are felt, but there is so much realistic and critical portraiture. The tradition of hagiography is not Jewish. Anyone who comes in contact with the Jewish Bible cannot take it as a pious document. It is a document of extraordinary revelation. I won't say it is a revelation of God, because that would only make me pious. But it is a record of religious reflection, often sharply satirical, towards a people bearing the promise and the blessing. Moses, for instance, is not allowed to enter the Holy Land. Moses's grave is unknown. There is no personality cult whatsoever, which is one reason why there could never be hagiography, except possibly in children's literature or educational material of the modern period. Every time you find a very strong personality, the Bible is wary. Think of the Patriarchs. Abraham is not depicted only in glowing terms. Perhaps the one who has the hardest time of it is Job, the perfect servant. Well, the perfect servant is humiliated, tested, tested again, just as Abraham was tested. No one is spared.

Biblical Judaism is a severe religion. God is jealous, and the demands are harsh. The Jews may be the "chosen" people, but "chosenness" here doesn't mean automatic preference or redemption. The covenant—being chosen or accepting it—is like a marriage. It's supposedly indissoluble. You have to live with God whether you like it or not. God is not described as fickle, but he has certain "emotions" and can get very angry indeed. You can put that down as anthropomorphism, but there's a strict and non-strict point of view about that "pathos." Maimonides in *The Guide for the Perplexed* maintains that even to say that God lives is anthropomorphism, for that "lives" is derived from an image of how we live. Yet without such "pathos," the Bible would be a book of laws instead of a book of the people.

You have edited a book about Bitburg, which is in part composed of press accounts of the controversy. Was the quality of the American press coverage of President Reagan's visit to the German cemetery of war dead, including S.S., with a mollifying and ahistorical statement—was that coverage adequate to the moral and social violations of the past and the present?

Both American and European accounts were of high quality. The incident showed the intersection of morality and politics in such a way that those who don't simply accept political expediency saw the problem emerge with a high degree of visibility. Politics became a kind of theater for issues that are with us all the time but don't achieve this degree of definition, for instance, the matter of reconciliation, or the relation of memory and offense. The individual has to live with offenses. We are insulted daily, whatever our group identity, Jew or non-Jew. What happened to the Jews in the Holocaust is seared in human consciousness. What happened is unforgettably inscribed on the survivors, and it has gradually penetrated those who didn't suffer it because they have begun to learn and to listen to the stories of the survivors. At the same time, a great many defense mechanisms come into play, because the Holocaust is such a terrible episode. One may understand this at an individual level in one's own life which is projected to the larger level of politics and history.

Bitburg raised the question of what reconciliation involves. Is forty years enough? Should statesmen or politicians arrogate to themselves the ability to say, "OK. That's enough"?

It's not that Germany hadn't been rehabilitated. Politically and economically it was rehabilitated long before Reagan planned the ceremonies at Bitburg. Nevertheless, the plan seemed to involve all kinds of intentions which pointed to the wish for an unwritten statute of limitations or a forced reconciliation: "We now have to close off this Nazi episode." So Bitburg raises the basic question of the American historical sense *and* the German historical sense.

Which of course involves literacy and the written word.

Indeed. The most articulate and interesting pieces in the collection have to do with the historical sense.

This is in the European press?

Yes, in the European press. Germany's own struggle with its historical past. On the other hand, the American press asked what kind of sense of history the American president had if he could gloss over things or be so selective. For me this became extremely important in terms of where we are as Americans, or as Europeans, in our attitude towards history. So the book is not only a collection of new essays. It also includes some of the best editorials and press articles in the United States, France, and Germany.

I also have an item from Russia. We usually say that it is the Russians who distort the past, who have a peculiar perspective, but in this case the distortion was on the side of the West.

Since the Holocaust was sustained—and partially incited—by vicious propaganda, by pseudohistory and a racist pseudobiology shaping those notions of pseudohistory, I think our obligation is to be very careful not to distort the past. With the best of intentions the president had allowed political expediency to foster a notion of the past that one could not permit to prevail. After the Holocaust we are on guard against versions of history that serve policy. Even as we realize that every "history" has a slant or bias, we build in a consciousness about that, a way of writing that makes one's position clear. To consecrate a false or simplified history by official statements and ceremonies cannot be passed by without protest. That would be unfaithful to Benjamin and his generation—a people hunted and slaughtered, two entire cultures, the Yiddish and the German-Jewish, almost cut off and existing now mainly in memory.

READINGS

Geoffrey Hartman's latest books include *Easy Pieces* (Columbia University Press, 1985), the editions of *Bitburg in Moral and Political Perspective* (Indiana University Press, 1986), *Shakespeare and the Question of Theory,* coedited with Patricia Parker (Methuen, 1985), and *Midrash and Literature,* coedited with Sanford Budick (Yale University Press, 1986). Aside from the articles appearing in the latter two volumes ("Shakespeare's Poetical Character in *Twelfth Night,*" and "The Struggle with Text"), his essay on "The Jewish Imagination" is in *Prooftexts* (Fall 1985). Two of his works dealing with recent criticism are *Saving the Text* (Johns Hopkins University Press, 1981) and *Criticism in the Wilderness* (Yale University Press, 1980). Among his other books are *The Unmediated Vision* (Yale University Press, 1954), *André Malraux* (Bowes and Bowes, 1960), *Beyond Formalism* (Yale University Press, 1970), *Wordsworth's Poetry* (Yale University Press, 1964), *The Fate of Reading* (University of Chicago Press, 1975). With David Thorburn he edited *Romanticism: Vistas, Instances, Continuities* (Cornell University Press, 1973). His poetry, *Akiba's Children,* was published by Iron Mountain Press in 1978.

J. HILLIS MILLER

I notice that most of your books are published by the Harvard University Press. Are you a "Harvard man"?

Harvard Ph.D., Oberlin undergraduate.

Your father was president of Keuka College and then moved to the Albany area. Was he associated with the State University of New York?

He was the Associate Commissioner for Higher and Professional Education in the state of New York at the time when the decision was made to diversify the state university, in 1948 or so. The question was whether they would have one massive university, or would they do what they had been doing. My father, perhaps when George Stoddard was still Commissioner, had a lot to do with making both the universities and the state colleges what they are today. SUNY-Albany was at that time a teachers' college.

This was under Governor Dewey?

Yes. My father was a southerner from Virginia, and the only time in his life that he ever voted for a Republican was in the 1948 presidential election. We were Democrats in upstate New York.

You were few.

Few and lonely. I can still remember the morning after the Alf Landon-Roosevelt race in 1936. To show what upstate New York was like, my friends and the parents of the students in the one-room school I went to were genuinely surprised that Landon had lost.

Almost without exception the parents would have voted for Landon?

So the only time my father ever voted for a Republican was when Dewey lost. He thought Dewey was O.K. Of course, I have just returned from Orange County, California, where the University of California at Irvine is located, and the Orange County Airport was renamed the John Wayne Airport, which is appropriate. That is where he lived and where his will was probated.

Who directed your dissertation at Harvard?

Douglas Bush.

Did you do work in the Renaissance?

No. Well, in a way. I had a very fine teacher at Oberlin named Andrew Bongiorno. He was an Aristotelian, and wanted me to go to Cornell to work with Lane Cooper and carry on in the tradition that he thought I ought to belong to. When he learned that I was going to Harvard anyway, he instructed me to work with Douglas Bush. So about the only way I remained faithful to Bongiorno was to have Bush direct a dissertation on Dickens, but not on the Renaissance at all.

Quite distant from Bongiorno's intention?

Of course there wasn't anyone like Bongiorno. He was a great teacher, is still a terrific teacher, and taught Renaissance literature, including Dante, and the history of literary criticism beginning with Aristotle. He thought it so important that I read Aristotle's *Rhetoric* that he tutored me for a whole semester, which I was very grateful for. Every week I would go to his house, and he would do another couple of chapters.

Did you take any courses in the classics?

Not there, no. If I had my life to live over again, Greek is what I would learn. I can make out in bilingual editions which word is which, but that's a far cry from reading Plato and Aeschylus and getting all the puns, or learning all the tenses, which are hideously difficult.

Where did you go after Harvard?

One year at Williams College, then to Johns Hopkins, where I was for nineteen years, and then here in '72.

There's a circuit, isn't there, between Yale and Johns Hopkins?

There's a circuit which is somewhat complicated, and it of course includes Cornell. Geoffrey Hartman and Paul de Man were both at Cornell. Paul went from Cornell to Hopkins. Geoffrey, originally at Yale, went to Cornell, and then came back here. But at the same time we were trying to hire Geoffrey at Hopkins, so that if he had not come here, he might conceivably have accepted a professorship at Hopkins.

Do you feel an identity with this group, Hartman, de Man, Bloom? Are there common characteristics of critical approaches, some common territories for you? They certainly aren't Aristotelians and neither are you.

No, not any more—although there are worse things one could read than Aristotle. I would rather be an Aristotelian than some things. I think, however, that these matters have more complicated histories than might first appear. I remember reading Geoffrey Hartman's first book when I was still at Harvard and being struck by it. I was doing criticism that was roughly phenomenological, influenced by Georges Poulet. I knew that someone else in America who was doing criticism that was in some way similar, to whom I could relate, was Geoffrey Hartman.

What book of his was this?

His dissertation, directed by René Wellek, *The Unmediated Vision*, has some historical importance as being one of the first books in America which showed some awareness of continental modes of criticism. That's partly due to Wellek and the breadth of the comparative literature program here and partly Geoffrey's own European background. The book is also a brilliant work in itself. Then the Wordsworth book came out. Of course, he lectured at Hopkins on Wordsworth before the book appeared in print. So that's a long kind of intellectual friendship.

In the case of de Man, it's different. I knew about him through Georges Poulet, who had been a professor at Hopkins and was the real source of my interest in continental criticism.

Haven't you done an essay on Poulet?

There's one on the Geneva school in general and another, a long essay, on Poulet, in a collection edited by John Simon. There's still another which set Poulet against Derrida published in *The Toronto Quarterly*.

But to return. I first heard of de Man, a brilliant critical writer, from Poulet, who was instrumental in getting him the professorship in Zurich. Poulet left Hopkins for Zurich, so there's another university involved in the intellectual circuit. I then met de Man here at Yale at a conference on criticism. Then, as now, he has the ability to deflect people's intellectual thinking. He does this with students and with colleagues. In my case very specifically this occurred. We were walking along the street talking about Heidegger. De Man in his cool, decisive way, said, "Really, you shouldn't spend much time on the later Heidegger. What you've got to do is read *Sein und Zeit*. That's the really crucial book." So we chatted a little about that. So I remember this as one of our first intellectual encounters. Then we succeeded in hiring de Man at Hopkins before he came here.

There were a lot of people responsible for my coming here, partly because Geoffrey and Paul were here already.

You mentioned the European background of Hartman and de Man. There are several questions to ask about that—first, the anxiety it creates in the American academic community. Generally the reaction

*has been antagonistic, both critically and journalistically. However,
let me reverse the question and turn it from those reviews and critical books and essays. Has the adverse reaction from a good many
of your national colleagues caused you to more closely communicate
and identify with one another here at Yale?*

There is a vague kind of solidarity in spite of the differences,
which I am sure some of the interviewees mentioned. All of us differ
in background and interest. I'm sure that Bloom talked about and
emphasized that he was not a deconstructionist. Geoffrey may have
said the same thing. Nevertheless, there were ways in which we all
found each other's work interesting, even in a negative way, and you
could say that all four of these people were doing something which
differed from, let's say, the Yale tradition of New Criticism, or from
Northrop Frye. At least in that sense we had some similarities, and
they preceded any gathering together to defend ourselves.

In fact it was the other way, the somewhat guileless self-group-
ing which called forth the wrath of the academicians. I say guileless
sincerely in the sense that one takes pleasure in having colleagues in
something that one is doing. It had never occurred to me that this
was a conspiracy or a gang of four. But there's obviously something
in the collective effect. If only one of us were here at Yale, and if
the others didn't know each other or were at other institutions, the
group would be less noticeable.

Of course, here at Yale, we are dispersed in the sense of be-
longing to different departments. We don't have a collective operation going. But outside it doesn't look that way.

The publications do all have Yale on them as a place of origin.

When I tell people that Geoffrey Hartman doesn't by any means
represent the Yale English department, the real temper or direction
of the department, and Harold Bloom is not in the English department, they don't believe me even though it's absolutely true.

Furthermore, I've been thinking of one feature of this "group-
ing." Two of the four are not Americans; they were born elsewhere
and have very different cultural backgrounds—de Man the only one
of the group with a real European education, and who for a period
functioned as a European intellectual, writing for European journals,
acting as a full professor in a European university, and so on. Geof-

frey was educated here, but nevertheless his early experience in England as an exile from Fascist Germany is important.

Bloom and I are the only Americans, "born and bred," but we differ in two ways that I think are important. Bloom's background is urban. Mine is rural. It's not that I'm a farmer—although both of my grandparents were farmers—but I lived outside major urban centers most of my early life. Delmar, New York, is not a city, and Keuka Park is not a city, and both of my grandparents came from small farms in Virginia. Oberlin, Ohio, is not a city but a small town.

I had never lived in a city until I went to Harvard, and I still remember the power of that experience. I went there in February, and there was snow on the ground. I walked up and down the streets of Cambridge. I had never been in something that was as much a kind of urban, intellectual center.

Whereas Harold comes from a very urban place, one of the New York boroughs. The shock for him was in going to Ithaca. Do you know the story of Bloom and the cow? The story, which he says is true, is that when he was at Cornell as a freshman he was out walking with another undergraduate, and Bloom said, "*What* is *that enormous* hairy animal?" The other person is supposed to have said, "Harold, that's a cow." He had never seen one. Opposed to Harold's Jewish background, which is increasingly important in his writing, and Geoffrey's, I'm from an American Protestant background. I come from a family that is mainly Pennsylvania Dutch on both sides, with some admixture of Scotch-Irish characteristic of Virginia farmer ancestry. My grandfather taught men's Bible school for twenty-five years, and knew the Bible inside and out—better than my father, a Baptist minister. I have a brother who is a Presbyterian minister. My mother is a Presbyterian. I was baptized at the age of twelve as a Northern Baptist. Although I'm not a very faithful inheritor of that tradition, it makes for a difference, my rural and Protestant background.

I've thought about why someone being that kind of American would have been attracted by, let's say, Derrida. I think I have an answer. There is a similarity between a certain aspect of American Protestantism, or even Protestantism generally, and the Jewish tradition, or the Jewish, intellectual European tradition, which is a suspicion of icons, of signs, of graven images, and a suspicion that things may not be for the best in the "best of all possible worlds," a kind of instinctive darkness of view, and a kind of conflict that I have in myself between a commitment to truth, the search for truth as the highest value, and moral values on the other. They may be in conflict. That is to say, you might reach a point where truth was challenging or dangerous to values.

So out of the Protestant tradition, there is on the one hand a commitment to truth-seeking and telling as the highest value, and on the other some kind of the sense of moral responsibility.

So the two have somehow a similarity for me. Kafka has always been very important to me. If Protestantism is taken one step further, there is a dubiety about the mediating power of anything, even Christ.

So the seeker, the messianic, must eventually come to an end?

That's what Protestantism has left; that is the rigorous kind of low Protestantism I was brought up in. It has Christ left, but has thrown all the rest away. What I was taught about the Bible, for example, was not exactly a fundamentalist or literal reading, but it was certainly not emblematic. All the richness of the Catholic tradition was missing. I was simply being taught how to find Habakkuk quickly.

Isn't the problem that language in dissenting Protestantism had to be controlled after the period of insurrection? One way of control would be a rigorous, dogmatic approach to language, the "literal" reading of the scriptures, or merely the rote learning and recitation of codified, carefully regulated texts. Isn't the problem this very misrepresentation of language itself?

That's right, but at least in my experience of American Protestantism, which involved Sunday school until I was in my teens, there was almost no theology taught at all, except as the simplest, barest kind of interpretation. The Lord's supper was taught as merely a commemorative operation, nothing about transubstantiation, consubstantiation. Just "Do this in commemoration of me." At the Northern Baptist church I went to there was simply a reenactment of that. It was not seen as having any efficacy beyond. It was only later, after that, that I learned there was anything to interpret. I was taught to make soap models of houses in Palestine and to find passages in the Bible, but not what they meant.

It's interesting. To some degree I have a kind of resentment against the American churches I went to for not having taught me anything about Christianity.

It's a coincidence that this came up. I began the interviews with Geoffrey Hartman, and the very question that we discussed was the problem, as I see it, of unstated Christian assumptions that find their way into criticism but are never recognized. What is consistently surprising is the absence of vocabulary, corresponding perhaps to the making of model houses of soap, which marks the critical enterprise.

But one should be aware, one should beware, that once you find something without stated assumptions it means that they are the latent ones which are just taken for granted. There may not be any overt metaphysics for criticism, yet there is one. One of the troubles we get into, one of the controversies we find ourselves in as critics, is by defining and calling these assumptions to notice. We have to ask serious questions. We make assumptions overt. A lot of people don't want to do that. Even Bloom himself will say he doesn't know anything about philosophy. What that means is not that he doesn't know philosophy, but that he doesn't want to discuss things at that particular level.

So when someone says he isn't a theoretician but just a practical critic, what that means is that he doesn't want the theoretical assumptions of the kind of criticism he does to be put into question or to be articulated. He doesn't think that he needs to. This is like the assumption, not at this university, but at many I know, that *one* theoretician is needed in a department, and that's enough.

The rest are "practical" critics?

The rest are something else, historians, practical critics; and English departments use this as an excuse not to hire any more of that kind of person: "We already have our theoretician." Whereas in fact all the other English department members are theoreticians too. A feature of literary study is that it must be based on theoretical presuppositions, either innocent or sophisticate.

In journalistic and scholarly criticism of the "Yale Critics" there is a good amount of abuse and misquoting. In Harry Levin's review of Gerald Graff's recent book, you are mentioned: "Hillis Miller performs the miraculous feat of cutting Dickens off from social reference (this was not a novel but reportage, 'Sketches by Boz')." Is this statement accurate?

First of all, that's Harry Levin on what, presumably, Graff has written.

Well, is the statement accurate?

What he does in this book is to pick an essay which wouldn't have occurred to me as an example of my most radical writing, which is an essay on Dickens and Cruikshank. It's on the illustrations of Dickens's first book, the *Sketches by Boz*, which are journalistic sketches. The essay was written quite a while ago and about two or three years before I came to Yale, '70 or '71. It's a long essay that was given at the Clark Library, UCLA. At any rate, there's no doubt that it was one of the early essays of mine which were in the new mode of criticism that I try to practice. I was trying to work out what is really problematic about the text of these sketches and the problem of "realism" particularly in relation to Cruikshank.

I don't think I said that Dickens is cut off from social reference. What I said was, there is a problem between the relationship of the purely literary aspect of those sketches, which in a later way anticipate Dickens's later work and what is poetic in that later work, both in the way in which the description of parts of London turn into stories, paradigmatic stories which are like *Oliver Twist* or like *Bleak House* already, and which are not, clearly, social reportage or stories which are not realistic and are not based on the preconceptions of the way life organizes itself in eighteenth-century description. There's a movement from marvelously lucid description and the way London looks. No one doubts that there really were old clothes shops in London at that time, but the transformation of that into something else, partly by these stories of Dickens and partly by figurative language, is not social realism.

The argument was that Cruikshank's pictures represent not at all the scenes in the stories of Dickens but are masterworks in the graphic tradition of Hogarth and Rowlandson. If you actually look at the *Sketches by Boz,* it's a vast oversimplification to say that Dickens started out as a journalist in the sense of someone who has done photographic representations of reality. That's the point of the essay. It's also interesting because of the generalizations that can be made about it. It's a straightforward essay.

I can see a subversive relation between text and illustration, insofar as the text comes from one tradition or a mixture of linguistic traditions and the pictures come from a tradition of graphic representation. They never quite get together. The Cruikshank pictures also contain something that is not in the text.

I understand that Graff's commitment is much different, a combination of Marx and Yvor Winters, who was his teacher. So he is most interested in preserving the referential ground of literature. Therefore, my essay would be particularly subversive in the view of those traditions because it puts "reference" in question. Graff wishes to *start* with the referential ground and go on from there. For me, representation is first of all a problem, maybe not irresolvable, but it isn't something that you can take for granted. The relation between a literary text and a nonlinguistic form of representation simply underscores the problem. So it's an oversimplification to say that my approach cuts Dickens off from social concerns.

Doesn't this get back to the problem of one word and one meaning, the still popular myth that each word is denotative in a simple, univocal sense? One of the reactions in eighteenth-century England to the danger of revolutionary seventeenth-century language was to restrict it to "literal" meaning and cast the heatedly propagandistic use of language, and by implication, poetic language, into the realm of the "unreasonable." Two questions then arose: the limitation of language to describe what occurs in actual usage; secondly, the overly inclusive use of terms such as ambiguity *or* irony *which hope to turn attention back to the text but which finally fail because of their inclusiveness.*

That would go along with what I was saying. The source, or the anxiety or antagonism in this particular case, is properly connected with the problem of referential language in the sense that if the possibility of correspondence between language and something which is not language is questioned, then the assumptions about determinate meaning go by the way.

So this would upset someone like Graff, who believes that language should accurately reflect the state of things as they are. If one is told that that is impossible, that there is no such language that can do that, then something has gone haywire with the whole enterprise, the whole validation of literature, both the grounds on which one decides whether there is a good piece of literature or a bad one.

An example of this social tendency in literature and criticism would be Lukács on Sir Walter Scott?

I guess it is in de Man's *Blindness and Insight* that one sees the point made about the conflict in the New Criticism between the commitment to referentiality, to moral values, the self-closure and homogeneity of the work, and the contradiction between those things and the insight offered by irony, which in fact is subversive.

Are there any American critics who precede you as examples?

If you have Kenneth Burke, you don't need either the New Criticism, or Todorov, or Roland Barthes, Raymond, or anybody else. It's all there but somewhat difficult to get out of Burke. One of his limitations, though Burke is a great critic, is the difficulty of getting out of him a practical procedure for teaching, for criticism, for interpreting works. One also finds that problem in Derrida, for example. But there's no doubt that the focus of our work, in one way or another, on figurative language and its role, is one of the things that troubles people.

Let me return to this. You were just speaking of figurative language, and there is a figure in Levin's review: "Professor Graff stands, like Dr. Johnson, ready to call us back to common sense by kicking the stone."

Well, you'd have to say that wasn't much of a refutation of Berkeley. Of course Bishop Berkeley left quite an academic legacy in this country, including his library and his name on Berkeley College here at Yale. I suppose that's what Harry Levin meant; there's some slight irony in that.

I was thinking more of the inadequacy of the analogy, the vulgar cartoon quality of it as a reduction of Johnson, once again, to an eccentric John Bull of letters, particularly when the incident is not characteristic of what Johnson wrote.

Well, it was a very striking gesture.

One that always is a capsule for Johnson, which disposes of him as a thinker, if not as a critic.

Could you comment on which writers and theoreticians introduced you to European philosophy?

I considered being a philosophy major at Oberlin, and had several courses in philosophy there, and have always been a reader of philosophy. So it's a matter of having an avocation for that all the time. So the connection between the philosophical and literary questions were made real for me not by Brooks and Warren, or even Ransom, but Empson, Burke, and Richards, and along with that, we began by talking about Aristotle.

This is not a trivial part of my education. After all, Aristotle demonstrated the connection between literary criticism and philosophy. I consider the presuppositions of literary criticism to be philosophical, metaphysical, even theological. They aid anyone in having thought-out solutions to the problems of criticism.

Readers generally have un-thought out appreciations of literature?

They may. Although I am skeptical about that. If your métier is to teach literature and to write about it, there is quite a different question, that of what is the adequate form of language with which to talk about books and literature.

And I should say something else. For the first two years in college I was a physics major, and I went to college intending to major in physics. I was very good in mathematics. It was only after two years there that I shifted to literature.

I can very distinctly remember the motivation was both a fascination for literature and the realization that that's what I really would prefer to do. But one aspect of the fascination with literature was about why people would write things that were so strange from the point of view of scientific language. Tennyson, I remember this very distinctly, seemed to me by most measurements of adequacy in language to be nonsense. Yet here was somebody I was told was a great poet. What was the explanation of this? How could somebody write like that and have it approved of by everybody? Now that's again a measure of the difference between me and Bloom, not to speak of the others.

Again, this is all rather odd. I did come from a professional family, but did grow up deprived of the great European and American tradition of poetry. Whereas Bloom was reading and memorizing Whitman at the age of eight.

Yet to some degree, it is still my motivation as a critic to "translate." When I get riled up about attacks of the sort we are talking about, I recall that most people in literature just don't realize how very strange the works of literature are. I still feel that. I'm still fascinated by that. If you just look at the works of literature in the most open and naive way, they are just very peculiar. They are like Southern California.

One of their peculiarities is the presence of figurative language. In any work of literature I know, once you get interested in that it's a lifetime project. And it seems to me that anyone's discourse about a great literary work is going to be reductive—but is calculated to cover over the genuine strangeness of literary works and to hide this from themselves and others. It may not always be good to know that kind of strangeness. It might be good, but there it is. There are those books. There is Tennyson, who still seems to me a very strange and strained mind. His greatness as a poet lies partly in that.

There's another point here that is interesting: namely, that the novel passes itself off, until recently, as being reality.

Yes. What I was talking about also seems to be the case about novels. Take the works of Anthony Trollope. I enormously admire his works.

Trollope is usually presented as a great novelist because he is "so realistic." He presents middle-class English life the way "it is." He is often admired by historians of the nineteenth century for that reason. He's an accurate reporter of courtship, marriage. There's been a highly successful TV series based on the Palliser novels. I do not deny that there is a sense in which all this is true. Trollope certainly understood social life and the class system of the British nineteenth century. And the reader, as with the great realists of the eighteenth century, gets accurate information.

Even in *Wuthering Heights,* which is not a realistic novel in the usual sense, I am persuaded that when Brontë describes the interior of a Yorkshire farmhouse, the open beams overhead with the hams hanging from them, that it is accurate. That is one of the reasons that one cherishes fiction.

I don't in any sense deny that aspect in literature in any form at all. There really are the mists of Lincolnshire for Tennyson. Nevertheless, when you get inside a Trollope novel, there are all sorts of things that by my measure are very odd. One of them is that the people always know what the other person is thinking, or at least to an extraordinary degree Trollope's characters are gifted with a kind of clairvoyance about the other person's mind. That is just not my experience with other people. Others are much more opaque than they are for Trollope in his fiction.

Part of the pleasure for me in reading him is almost that of science fiction. There's a pleasure in entering the kind of universe where people have a system of thought perception, a manner of thought perception, a gift which you can say Trollope justifies by having all of the characters from the same village who accept the same assumptions. That may be a measure of the difference between a late twentieth century American and a mid–Victorian Englishman.

But I'm not so sure of how one would test that. I don't think it can be tested merely by saying that Trollope knew the habits of courtship and was sociologically accurate. Yet that aspect of the novels, the degree to which the characters really know what's going on, that they are supposed to tell a reader what's going on in society, is there.

Well, that's the complaint, that there's more going on in the fiction than in your reading.

But I think the test of these questions is the texts. The question is which account of Trollope's novels, critically, is most adequate. In that sense I still believe in verification and validity in a careful and calculated way. But when I say a work is undecidable or open-ended, that does not mean that there is not a better or worse reading of the novel. In fact, criticism is meant to be a very definite act that is as specific as possible, that concerns a very specific form of alternating meaning, or undecidable meaning, which can be manifested by citations and discussion. The indeterminacy can be determined, to some degree, by those means.

I think the test of these questions is the texts. The question is which account of Trollope's novels is more adequate to those texts, and in that sense I still believe in verification and validity. The text would still have to be defined in a careful and calculated way.

So when I say that a work is undecidable or open-ended, that does not mean that there's not a better or worse reading of the novel. In fact, my discussion is meant to be as exact a discussion as possible, and the limits of the parts of the discussion that are open-ended are to be as exact as possible. Their interdeterminacy can be determined by discussion and citation.

This is an important and often misunderstood point.

One can see why, but when de Man or I use the term indeterminacy it means the alternation between specific possible meanings between which the text doesn't allow a decision. It's understood, rather, to mean that the meaning of the text is imposed on it by the reader.

This is the basis of my animus toward reader-response criticism, which in good hands like Stanley Fish's doesn't really mean that, but sounds like that: Here's the text, and everybody sees it differently. Students will all too easily fall into that kind of perspectivism because it's built into the subject-object dichotomy learned from the New Criticism. Our criticism would seem to say, therefore, that there is no way to distinguish between one reading and the quality of a text compared with another.

This quite properly upsets people because it appears to take away authority. But to fall back on a somewhat naive notion, the only other possibility, opposing such apparent chaos, is *single meaning*, a closed text, an organic structure, and all that. That now seems naive in the extreme simply because it ignores the nature of language.

So I would say that the test, though it's a very hard one to apply because people will go on disagreeing and saying you're wrong about this or that text—nevertheless, the ultimate appeal is to the adequacy of the interpretation. For me to speak about deconstruction as a mode of interpretation which presupposes the possible heterogeneity of a text, whether philosophical, literary, or critical, deconstruction is simply a feature of language—of writing and reading.

Deconstruction simply supposes, because of the nature of language, that any one of those texts is not going to be dismantled by somebody else, but that they already dismantle themselves. It's simply impossible to define the text, or language, as one simple thing without someone being able to point to things in the text which contradict it.

That's the hypothesis. That's the feature of language in general and of literary language, and the easiest way to talk about the features of language is through figures of speech. So it's not a matter of the critic deconstructing, but of claiming that the text deconstructs itself. All you have to do is to follow the lines of this definition, which means paying attention to features of the text which had been arbitrarily passed over to make single claims for meaning. Deconstruction in denying the single meaning of texts is a more adequate account of that strangeness I was talking about. Yet, I'm still true to the New Criticism, the kind of inheritance that I have, in that ultimately my real interest is in accounting for literary texts.

So when I say that criticism is a form of literature, it doesn't mean that the critic arrogates to himself some vague poetic power. It means that there's no language of criticism that can escape the problems of language the poet himself faced. There is no metalanguage, or purely rational language, or language which is a tool of command, a sort of sovereign control of the text.

So it's meant to be a statement of humility rather than the other way around in the sense which says, if George Eliot had these problems, or Wallace Stevens, or Trollope, how can I, a critic, expect to do them one better at their own game? Presumably, if they had been able to put things straight, they would have done so.

However, the artist supposedly removes one level of ambiguity about experience. The reader looks at a work of literature and finds a greater degree of unity than in mere, unconnected experience?

What I'm saying is that unity isn't there and it can be demonstrated not to be there. The attraction or fascination for me in this kind of criticism is that it does seem to account for more features that are objectively there in the literary text than other critical presuppositions.

I mentioned George Eliot's *Middlemarch*. It's often been said that there is a control, an organization, an organic wholeness in that work. There are several brilliant articles that argue this.

Now that has its virtues, because it at least leads a reader to look for connections. I used to argue with my old colleague Earl Wasserman at Johns Hopkins who was an intellectual and a "unifier." Earl and I had a dialogue about these matters for nineteen years from the time I came to Hopkins until the time I left. He was a very important person in my thinking, partly because he disagreed in a fruitful way. Earl used to say, quite properly, that the assumption of organic unity led the reader to assume that every part of the text was going to have meaning. There's something to that.

Let's take that a little bit further. Assume that there is a plant— there is of course all of the literature from the eighteenth century about plants, including Erasmus Darwin's long poem—if the flower is taken and analyzed, the parts do have to be there, and each contributes to the flower itself, and this forms the analogy for wholeness and meaning in language. However, in literature it's not just a plant, but language that is being analyzed?

That's the problem. A critic may illicitly transpose a structure made of words, with the specific problems inherent in language, for something that is not a sign but an object. This then allows the reader to import all sorts of additional metaphors, such as the genetic one. There was a seed and it grew and so on. Because of the originally simple analogy with the plant, there are elaborate presuppositions which avoid essential questions and bypass the obvious fact that literature is verbal, not physical.

So I think that what would be more to the point as a challenge to this notion of criticism would be an attempt to refute the readings that arise on the basis of such suppositions. Then you would have form where you could talk about the text and all the problems that there are—you read one, I read one, everybody reads one differently. Nevertheless, there would be something there, the words, and at least we could talk about them to more point than by merely saying they are organic.

To put it another way, there would be ways of attacking Geoffrey Hartman, Harold Bloom, or myself, or de Man. But for the most part it hasn't been well done. The way to do it would be to demonstrate details of our readings and to demonstrate that they are false. Using Bloom as an example, the real interest of Bloom to me is not the twelve tropes, or the twenty-five tropes, or whatever they are, but he seems to tell me things in his critical writing about texts that are really there, about Tennyson, for instance, that no one has really said before.

The same thing goes for Derrida. His essay on Plato is amazing in that it is a real piece of interpretation of Plato's text.

The only way to refute it, I think, is not to say that deconstruction is nonsense, or it's immoral and is going to lead to the end of the western world, but to show that's not what Plato's text means. Now one might be able to do that, but nobody has ever really tried.

That would be a real challenge.

So what really interests me is not the theory itself, but in establishing some kind of tools, or ability, to make an adequate report on what's actually there in a piece of literature. This kind of criticism at this moment seems to me to do this better than any other.

Yes, but what's wrong with saying that literature is, or can in some cases be "realism," or literature is history, or literature is a revelation of the self?

Well, I have some sympathy for those who find the approach ultimately tedious, or reductive, to be told that all literature is about itself, that it has as its subject matter only language. That may be true, but the other approaches aren't going to entice too many young people into reading *Paradise Lost*. So you can take any one of these approaches you mentioned and make them problems rather than presupposed answers. If you suppose that literature is going to teach something the reader doesn't already know, it would be perfectly all right to start out by saying that literature is realism, and then leave the notion of *realism* and how it functions open for a while as something that you were going to test out with the works. That would be fine. And that's true for the other approaches.

I often have the feeling with students that they have good ideas about literature, but they don't carry them far enough. The problems they have is not that they haven't fruitful hypotheses, but that they don't develop them. They haven't learned to say, "If this is the case, then where does it lead, or what conclusion can be drawn, what does it say about this, what about that?" So it may be that those things that connect literature with things outside itself are a good place to begin rather than to just be blandly told that literature is just about language.

But insofar as being human—as Kenneth Burke says, man is a symbol-using animal, and being human involves being permeated with language through and through. So linguistic questions are there for life.

However, you wouldn't want literature to take on everything. I think that's the problem. Departments of English teach psychology, sociology, etc., and students flock to such courses to talk about people, about themselves, and about society. Whereas the specific feel for literature obviously has to do with the kind of language, the relation of certain kinds of language, to these problems.

So there is nothing in practice which prevents a student from studying "realism" or "history" in literature as well as theories of deconstruction?

That's right. Moreover, if you carried these questions further you would come to the issue of how literature represents the self. You would then study literature with this in mind and discover that it is the relation of selfhood and language.

If one were to read a translation of Thucydides, for instance, the presence of the translator is explicitly present in the text, which is, of course, "history."

Insofar as the colleges and universities are based on the idea of translatability of language, insofar as we are still, generally, a monolingual culture, insofar as the humanities are the supporters of that idea in the university, the scientists might well say, "What are those fellows doing over there in the humanities?" The response is, "They are upholding humanistic values." We do this, primarily, by teaching things in English *and* in translation. No one knows Greek or reads

Aristotle in Greek except a few specialists. Most departments of English, including this one, are in practice departments of comparative literature in translation. One of the major courses at Yale for undergraduates is English 129, "World Literature," and there are many others here involving the same approach.

Now, insofar as attention to figurative language and other linguistic problems puts in doubt the possibility of translation—really puts it in doubt, which it surely does, and raises questions about translatability, then the whole structure of the university is obviously in danger.

However, the humanities are built on an assumption that for all practical purposes one can take a course in the history of philosophy in English translation. You know that the texts were written in Latin and other languages, but you wouldn't teach it in those original texts.

That's one of the points made by W. K. C. Guthrie, who discusses Greek philosophical words that have been translated as vague terms of Whiggery and moral improvement. Again, these translations, or mistranslations, have been implicit. None of the examples he uses were the results of intentional mistranslation. They were all unrecognized, all implicit.

This is Heidegger's complaint about the translation of the Greek *logos* into the Latin *ratio,* which is something very different.

But to conclude, one of the things that supports this kind of criticism, represented by the concern for language itself, is that we are becoming, the United States is becoming, a multilingual culture. More and more people are becoming aware of this in practical ways, such as "English as a second language" in university courses, or the discovery that English itself has its own nontranslatable idioms. Also, there are many more people now who know foreign languages than was the case before.

There's one other negative treatment of the European and European-related critical enterprise I would like to ask you about. Hayden White in an essay published in Directions for Criticism *questions the critical undertaking by a minority of you at Yale.*
Please give me your reaction to this:

To be sure, most critics—what we should call Normal critics—
continue to believe that literature not only has sense but makes
sense of experience. Most critics continue to believe, accordingly,
that criticism is both necessary and possible. Normal criticism is
not a problem, then—at least, of Normal critics. Their problem
is Absurdist criticism, which calls the practices of Normal criti-
cism into doubt. It would be well, of course, for Normal critics
to ignore their Absurdist critics, or rather their Absurdist meta-
critics—for Absurdist criticism is more about criticism than it is
about literature.

Two things strike me as being wrong about this, first, the term
absurdist is misleading in the sense that nothing could be more
rational, more in control, more a product of intelligence at a high
level than de Man's work, Bloom's work, or Derrida's work, and
intelligence of that kind has some of the inevitable strangeness that
literature itself has. It's not surprising that minds of that level produce writing that is at times difficult to understand.

But that it is irrational? The very topics critics deal with baffle
the mind to the extent that those who try to use the traditional
terms of rationality undertake a very nearly impossible task. So to
call the critics "absurdist"? It is not like reading an essay by a
dadaist, or by Beckett, even. The writing just isn't like that.

Another very important point is that critical writing should be
measured by the validity and accuracy of what is said about literature, not that they talk about themselves or make metacritical points.
The test, the real interest, of these critics is what de Man tells me
about a passage in Proust that I wouldn't have been able to figure
out for myself, and the way he makes the distinction between one
figure of speech and another for the interpretation of a passage.

White continues: "There has always been an impulse in criticism to
view the text as, according to Hillis Miller, the Geneva School critic
Beguin views it: as a sacrament that bears 'precious witness . . . of
god's presence in creation.'"

He's identifying me with an earlier essay I wrote. There's been
a shift in my work since then, although I still remain fundamentally
interested in language and consciousness.

But what you were saying about "normal" critics wanting literature to "make sense"—I think that these critics want it to make

sense too. Bloom, certainly, talks about literature as an expression of life-situations, and so in a way does de Man. What he says at the end of one of his essays, to paraphrase, that literature *can't* say what it means, has consequences for life. Well, he's of course talking about literature and its relation to human life itself.

So I don't think I or my colleagues can be attacked on those grounds. One could get at us on the grounds that the picture of life that we find in literature is not the one that literature actually expresses, that it is not as troubling as in fact it is and remains.

But to come back again to this point: the obligation to actually report what readers find in literature is more important than to make sure that they find something elevating or life-sustaining in the conventional optimistic way.

Isn't there uncertainty in your critical stance that readers would not welcome? A good many students prefer definite answers—a process of information.

Well, it could be introduced gradually, such as a discussion of ambiguity, irony, paradox in the early stages of the course. However, a critic doesn't know where this will lead, any more than does a scientist. Maybe if we took another approach, that of science, we would be better off. Science would not make advances if it had as a presupposition that what it was going to find was going to be benign. It believes that it is better *to know*.

So this might take me back to what I was saying about Protestantism, which began with the assumption that it was better to know the truth, no matter what darkness that led you to, than to fool yourself.

You are not then, technicians talking to other technicians?

Well, look, the teaching of literature either technically or commonly is not in all that great shape at many institutions of higher learning. It happens to be in very good shape here, but I'm told, when I go around the country, the enrollments in English are going down. So it means not only the shift to expository writing, but that people, somehow, don't view the study of Shakespeare and Milton as valuable in this country, or *as* valuable. There's doubt about it.

So I would not say that the changes in the curriculum made in response to different and new interests are those of technocrats, but they are the reverse. In other words, I would make claims for the teachability of this approach to literature, and its ability to deal concretely with works of literature and to make them available to students.

Nevertheless, I have the feeling that for the public mind, what we're talking about is teaching people how to write clearly, meaning, again, one word corresponding to a single, unambiguous meaning. In other words, the presupposition of the "back to basics" is the idea of language mentioned earlier. Insofar as language doesn't work that way, this assumption will make for problems in expository writing programs.

So I would see a very fruitful interchange going on between expository writing, which I view as a very important discipline, and rhetoric as a study of deconstruction, of the study of figurative language. In the immediate future, there should be a very fruitful exchange between these disciplines, which will in turn help to bring literary study and expository writing together, and keep them together where they should be. Writing and reading are intimately related.

More often than not, the bias of a work can be determined by its title, such as the "function" of literature, which is the analogy of something mechanical or hygienic. What about The Form of Victorian Fiction?

That's a transitional book which was written in 1968, and there's the Hardy one after that. So those books are dialogical in the sense that they are on the brink of the direction my later critical viewpoint and writing took.

The notion of history in the earlier works, the idea of *Zeitgeist*—something specific about Victorian literature—I would now find an unsatisfactory notion. It's not that there is no such thing as literary history. The redefinition of what that is, is now one of the major problems of critical and scholarly writing. But I would now be inclined to see this as a way of arranging material in a specific time—materials or elements that are really universal.

However, Marxism or some form of sociology of literature is one of the strongest alternatives to deconstruction at this moment.

One of the points made in attacks on Derrida is that he deals with masterworks of the western tradition, invents something called "logocentric metaphysics," which is atemporal. He ignores history. That is a serious challenge. However, it depends on what one means by the term *history*.

But where I would differ with Marxism, as I understand it, is not about the specificity about the English eighteenth or nineteenth centuries, but that the period is *not determined* by the material means of production, although they are a part of the period.

So the Zeitgeist *is not determined by account books, personal diaries, or industrial records?*

That's right. It's rather a matter of arrangement of materials, of elements that are universal to our tradition, and which if not linguistically determined are easier to identify, such as the concept of selfhood.

Another way to put this would be to say that even in human history, or prehistory, which has gone on for thousands of years, a couple of millennia aren't really long enough to produce radical changes in human nature and human experience. The evidence for this is how familiar Plato is to us, or even Shakespeare. There is some advantage to taking an approach that discusses what is familiar in writers, their use of language, rather than what I was taught: that Shakespeare is so strange and believed such crazy things that you have to read Tillyard's *Elizabethan World Picture*. So it's almost like a branch of anthropology: Elizabethan literature is so strange; it therefore is implicitly irrelevant.

Whereas the concept of variations within a culture which has remained to a considerable degree the same, the same kind of terms, the same kind of assumptions, makes western culture much more available, makes Ben Jonson a kind of contemporary.

That's an advantage of the criticism we must express.

What's occurred recently as a reaction to what Derrida, you, and others do under the loose title of "deconstruction"?

Not long ago Paul de Man could cheerfully say, with how much or how little irony it is impossible to know, that *the* task of criticism in the coming years would be a kind of imperialistic appropriation of all of literature by the method of rhetorical reading often called "deconstruction."

In fact there has been a massive shift of focus in literary study since 1979 away from the "intrinsic" rhetorical study of literature toward study of the "extrinsic" relations of literature, its placement within psychological, historical, or sociological contexts. There has been a shift away from an interest in "reading," which means a focus on language as such, its nature and powers, to various forms of hermeneutic interpretation, which means focus on the relation of language to something or other, God, nature, society, history, the self, outside language. There has been a tremendous increase in the appeal of psychologistic and sociological theories of literature such as Lacanian feminism, Marxism, Foucaultianism, along with a wide-spread return to old-fashioned biographical, thematic, and literary historical methods that antedate the New Criticism and are often blithely carried on as if the New Criticism, not to speak of more recent rhetorical methods, had never existed. This geological slippage or drift is as much visible on the "right" as on the "left." Both sides maintain that the era of "deconstruction" is over. It has had its day, and we can return with a clear conscience to the real lives of men and women in society as they exist in themselves and as they are "reflected" in literature. We can ask again pragmatic questions about the uses of literature in human life and in society. We can return, that is, to what the study of literature has always tended to be when it is not accompanied by serious reflection on the specificity of literature as a mode of language. According to their negative critics, de Man or Derrida make such extravagant demands on the mere act of reading a poem, a novel, or a philosophical text that it makes one tired just to think of it. Surely reading cannot be all that difficult! Or require such self-consciousness, such hesitations! Surely no one can be expected to master the intricate rigor of the deconstructive way of reading and apply it habitually. We need to get on with it. Taking seriously what deconstruction says about the language of literature or about language as such might cause an indefinite delay or postponement of our desire to turn our attention to the relations of literature to history, to society, to the self. De Man has, in what is already a classic essay on the topic, "The Resistance to Theory," in a 1982 issue of *Yale French Studies,* analyzed the reasons for this impatience, this collective desire to repress, to evade the difficulties of seeing literature clearly and thinking out rigorously its nature as a specific use of language. It is proof of what de Man says in the essay that the essay itself was rejected for inclusion in a volume sponsored by the Modern Language Association of America on the relations of literary study to other disciplines. Apparently de Man's theory of the resistance to theory met considerable resistance.

An editorial task performed, no doubt, fairly and without prejudice?

Not at all. The shift away from the rhetorical study of literature is often accompanied by a false account of what is actually said about the extrinsic relations of literature by de Man or Derrida. These critics are said to be concerned only with language, even to cut language off from the real world of history and of living men and women. Deconstruction is lumped with other outmoded, sterile, and elite formalisms. It is opposed to the newer sociological methods which are pragmatically engaged in the real world outside language.

The question is what these methods have to do with the study of literature? It is in defining that liaison that the difficulties and disagreements begin. My contention is that the study of literature has a great deal to do with history, society, the self, but that this relation is not a matter of thematic reflection within literature of these extralinguistic forces and facts. Rather it's a matter of the way the study of literature offers perhaps the best opportunity to identify the nature of language as it may have effects on what de Man called "the materiality of history." Here "reading," in the sense of a rhetorical analysis of the most vigilant and patient sort, is indispensable. How else are we going to know just what a given text is and says, what it can do? This can never be taken for granted beforehand, not even after that text has been overlaid by generations of commentary.

Since "reading" in this sense is indispensable to any responsible concern for the relations of literature to what is outside it, it would be a catastrophe for the study of literature if the insights of deconstruction, along with those of the New Criticism and of such critics as Empson and Burke, were to be forgotten or were to be relegated to an overpassed stage in some imagined historical "development," so that they no longer need to be taken seriously in the actual, present-day work of literary study. I should go so far to say that, to paraphrase de Man, the task of literary criticism in the coming years will be in mediation between the rhetorical study of literature, of which "deconstruction" is by far the most rigorous in recent times, and the now so irresistibly attractive study of the extrinsic relations of literature. Without the rhetorical study of literature, focused on language, its laws, what it is, and what it can do, particularly on the role of figurative language in interfering with the straightforward working of grammar and logic, we can have no hope of understanding just what the role of literature might be in society, in history, and in individual human life.

In our anxiety to make the study of literature count we are always in danger of misplacing that role, of claiming too much for literature, for example, as a political or historical force, or of thinking of the teaching of literature as too explicitly political, in the sense that the work of a member of Congress is political or in the sense that I commit a political act when I vote. No one can doubt that literature is performative, that it makes things happen, that it is a way of doing things with words, and no one can doubt that the teaching of literature always has a political component, perhaps most when I am most silent about its political implications, ignorant of them or indifferent to them. It is not so much that the performative effects of literature, for better or for worse, are overestimated, as that they are often located in the wrong place. Sociological theories of literature which reduce it to being a mere "reflection" of dominant ideologies in fact tend to limit its role to that of passive mirroring, a kind of unconscious anamorphosis of the real currents of power.

De Man was always interested in such dualisms, even while he attempted to reveal their basic simplicity?

De Man went so far as to say that *rhetorical complexity generates history.* So it is in fact not the case that the work of de Man or Derrida is entirely "intrinsic," entirely concerned with language as such, limited to language in rarefied isolation from the extralinguistic. There is a fully elaborated theory of the historical, psychological, and ethical relations of literature in de Man's *Allegories of Reading.* Work he was doing in the last two or three years of his life was increasingly focused on such questions, no doubt as one more example of that almost universal shift to politics, history, and society which marks the current moment in literary study. In that essay I mentioned entitled "The Resistance to Theory," for example, de Man says that rhetorical study of literature contributes to social, political, and historical understanding.

One may wish to argue or to say that de Man got the relation of the study of language and literature to politics all wrong, but only in bad faith could one say he does not explicitly account for the political and historical implications of his theory of language and of what he calls "literariness." Or rather it would be better to speak of what he has written not as abstract theory but as praxis, since almost all of his work centers on the reading of some text or other, for example, the series of essays on different works by Rousseau in *Allegories of Reading*. Or rather, to refine still further, what he has written, like all good literary study, is neither pure theory nor pure praxis, "practical criticism," nor yet a mixture of the two or something between the two, but a mode of interpretative language which is beyond that false and misleading opposition. One might call it "exemplification," but that would leave open the question, "exemplification of just what?" The answer must be that each good example of reading is an exemplification of other examples, according to a strange logic of synecdoche in a situation like literary study in which no possibility of totalization or the establishment, once and for all, of an all-encompassing general theory exists. If, in any case, one of the simultaneously practical and theoretical dimensions of Paul de Man's work is a scrupulous accounting for the referential, historical, social, and political effects of literature, the same thing can just as decisively be demonstrated for Jacques Derrida, who has all along included consideration of the institutional, political, and social implications of his work, for example in *Positions,* or, more recently, in an interview entitled "Deconstruction in America" in a 1985 issue of *Critical Exchange.*

That the opponents of the rhetorical study of literature from both sides of the political spectrum continue to misrepresent it as ahistorical and apolitical may indicate the importance of what is in question here. The stakes, one can see, are enormous, both for literary study as such and for the function of literary study in society as it is now and as it is likely to be in the coming years, in continuing to think out the implications of the rhetorical study of literature for the political and ethical life.

What's the subject of your most recent work?

My own work recently has been concerned with what I call "the ethics of reading." I propose to exemplify my claim that the rhetorical study of literature is deeply committed to taking seriously the so-called extrinsic relations of literature by a further exploration of this topic.

Is there an ethical dimension to the act of reading as such? Of course, I mean "reading" itself, not the expression of ethical themes in a text.

Reading might seem to be initially and perhaps primarily a matter of getting the meaning of what is read right, that is, a cognitive or epistemological matter, not an ethical matter having to do with conduct and responsibility. Nevertheless, just as Henry James in the eloquent paragraph which ends the preface to *The Golden Bowl* claims that the act of writing is a privileged part of what he calls "the conduct of life," so I claim that the act of reading too is part of the conduct of life. My ethical act as reader, moreover, would have the most extensive practical consequences of an ethical, institutional, and political sort. My recommendation is that we should give up the attempt to transfer ethical themes directly from literature to life. It would follow that departments of literature should reduce their function to a kind of linguistics, that is, to a study of the rhetoric of literature, what might be called "literariness."

What future do you see for the methods of reading you have been describing? For instance, would or can deconstruction itself be institutionalized?

I don't think so. The rhetorical study of literature is eminently teachable, if there happen to be teachers to teach it—no small *if*. On the other hand it is in principle impossible to institutionalize deconstruction in the ordinary sense, to make it into a "method" with practical rules and procedures that can be passed on from teacher to student. The study of the rhetoric of literature is not a "method" of reading in this sense. As soon as deconstruction is formalized in this way, it is no longer deconstruction. It is dead. This is surely one of the dangers it faces today. Deconstruction is allergic to institutionalization, to being made a method.

But there are in fact acolytes of deconstruction in the academy. So where does your discussion leave those who teach?

The teaching of reading in the sense of knowledge of the rhetoric of literature, deconstructive or not, always occurs fortuitously. It does not go without saying that it is a good thing that it should happen, but it happens when it happens, when there is someone in a "teaching position" who for some reason knows how to read or learns how to do it and is able to convey that by exemplification to students, *not* by the teaching of theory as such. Reading "otherwise" or "allegorically," that is, reading "reading," always occurs against the grain of the institutional context in which it happens. It therefore can occur anywhere at any time, in any department or in any program in any school, college, or university, perhaps best in those that are least hospitable to it, though in such cases, of course, censorship of one sort or another is always likely to silence it.

The future of literary studies in America depends on the fact that in our colleges and universities that silencing is far less likely to happen than in many countries, even if it ironically often fails to happen as a result of a secret and mistaken conviction that, in any case, nothing "politically" important is taking place or could take place in departments of literature. So it would be beneficial to the health of our society to have an abundance of good readers. I would go so far as to say it would bring a millennium—the millennium of good readers—the end of wars and of class conflict, a reign of justice, peace, and happiness. That this millennium like others is exceedingly *un*likely to occur is not incompatible with my conviction that one of the major tasks of higher education in the next century will be to foster conditions in which good reading as I have defined it is likely to happen.

I would like to conclude on a more immediate and less abstract level. What's the relation between teacher and text? Is it "ethical," "practical," what?

First, I think that the primary ethical obligation of the teacher of literature is to the work of literature. If there is a conflict between that and the teacher's obligation to students, in one direction, and to the institution, in the other, the obligation to the work takes precedence by an implacable law of reading. Though one can imagine a situation in which a teacher might choose to remain silent about what she or he has seen in a work by not teaching that work, if she or he teaches the work at all, they must tell it like it is. The whole sequence of obligations begins with the act of reading and with the call or demand which the work makes on its reader. Good reading means noncanonical reading, that is, a willingness to recognize the unexpected, perhaps even the shocking or scandalous, present even in canonical works, perhaps especially in canonical works, in Homer, Dante, or Shakespeare, in Milton or Wordsworth, even in Matthew Arnold himself, for example in his *Empedocles on Etna* or in those strange books on the Bible he wrote at the end of his life. By a noncanonical reading I do not mean a critical relativism or a placing of meaning in the "reader's response," a freedom to make the work mean anything one likes, but just the reverse. I mean a response to the demand made by the words on the page, an ability, unfortunately not all that common, to respond to what the words on the page say rather than to what we wish they said or came to the book expecting them to say.

Good reading does not occur all that often, not as often as one might perhaps expect or wish. Perhaps it occurs most often in those who are also good writers. Good reading is by no means a direct result of the reader's theoretical presuppositions. Literary theory may help or inhibit good reading, but woe to the reader who goes to a work simply to find confirmation of her or his theory. They will certainly find what they seek, but will not have read the work. Good reading is more likely to lead to the disconfirmation or severe modification of a theory than to offer any firm support for it. So reading, not theory, is the one irreplaceable necessity in the teaching of literature. The rare ability to see the object, in this case a poem, a novel, a play, or a work of philosophy, as in itself it really is, to borrow Arnold's phrasing again, is the one thing necessary in the good teacher of literature. The strangest and most surprising things are present if we have the wit to see them. The canonized classics remain in the libraries and bookstores, or on our own shelves at home, like so many unexploded time bombs ready to go off when there is the conjunction of the work and the good reader of that work. Such conjunctions make something happen and have their ethical effects, but exactly what these may be can never be certainly predicted.

My second conviction about the new ethics of reading is that its primary obligation will be or ought to be philological. The teaching of literature must be based on a love for language, a care for language and for what language can do. The study of literature must begin with language and remain focused there. Its primary tools are citation and discussion of that citation. Such study must be a rhetoric and a poetics before it is literary history or a repertoire of the ideas which have been expressed through the centuries in literature. The necessity of this primary focus on language as such is perhaps the most controversial of the assertions I am making here. Perhaps it is too much to expect departments of English and the other modern languages not to teach everything under the sun, but to return to their primary subject matter and to concentrate on their real business of teaching good reading. But since good reading is fundamentally necessary to good writing, such an apparent narrowing of scope would have the virtue of bringing together the teaching of reading and the teaching of composition. Moreover, it is only on the basis of the knowledge of what language is and what it can do, what we can do with it and what we cannot do with it, that it is possible to move on to those questions I began by asking about the role of literature in private and social morality, in history, and in the making of public policy.

Finally, even though I may repeat myself, there is a third feature of the new ethics of reading as I foresee it. We may rejoice that the United States is well on the way to recognizing that it is a multilingual not a monolingual country. We may rejoice also that impressive advances in the teaching of languages have been made and incorporated into many secondary school curricula. Some students actually come to college now knowing a second language well. Also, there has been a shift in the center of gravity of literary study away from the national literatures studied separately to one form or another of comparative literature or of interdisciplinary study. The new forms of this, however, would put in question the idea of translatability which was often a presupposition of older forms of comparative literature. Translation is now seen as a problem, a topic of fundamental importance to be studied, not a solution.

The new rhetoric and poetics therefore presuppose a fundamental untranslatability from language to language. They might take Walter Benjamin's "Die Aufgabe des Übersetzers" as a signal text for beginning to understand why this is so as a fact about language. This does not mean that it is not better to read Homer or Dante, Descartes or Hegel, Tolstoi, Baudelaire, or Benjamin himself in the best translation available—but how would one know—rather than not read them at all, just as those who do not read Greek should read Milton or Wordsworth. *It does mean* that readers can never trust a translation any more than they can trust what secondary books or teachers say is going on in a given work of literature or philosophy. If you are to have a hope of finding this out you must read the work in the original. This obligation of the reader to respond to the demand made by the text remains the primary imperative in the ethics of reading.

READINGS

J. Hillis Miller is the author of *Charles Dickens* (1958), *The Disappearance of God* (1963), *Poets of Reality* (1965), *Thomas Hardy* (1970), *Fiction and Repetition* (1982), all published by Harvard University Press; *The Form of Victorian Fiction* (1968) by the University of Notre Dame Press; *The Linguistic Moment* (1985) by Princeton University Press; *The Ethics of Reading* (1986) by Columbia University Press). Among his many articles are "Character in the Novel: A Real Illusion," in *From Smollett to James*, edited by Samuel I. Mintz et al. (University of Virginia Press, 1981); "The Disarticulation of the Self in Nietzsche," *Monist* 64 (1981); and "The Geneva School: The Criticism of Marcel Raymond, Albert Béguin, Georges Poulet, Jean Rousset, Jean-Pierre Richard, and Jean Starobinski," *Critical Quarterly* 8 (1966), reprinted in *Modern French Criticism*, edited by John K. Simon (University of Chicago Press, 1972).

PAUL DE MAN

*L*et me ask you about your work on the concept of irony. There's a notorious exchange in a Hemingway novel when one of the characters thumbs his nose at the mention of the term. This may have been an oddity of response during the 1920s, but the same reaction no longer holds true, certainly, today. Why should irony, this emphasis on doubleness, tripleness, be so prominent in recent discussions of literature?

You speak of doubleness, tripleness, and so on, and you immediately ask the question in a historical context by asking what has happened now that irony is again emphasized. That's surely not the case—whether there is now more emphasis or less emphasis on irony, and how you would measure just how much irony. You know, you can't be a "little bit ironic."

But nevertheless, what you speak of is true in a sense. What you are speaking of is a certain degree of self-consciousness, self-awareness, doubleness, and one always assumes this in any critical enterprise, because it is in the nature of that enterprise to work on something that already comes to you so that you have the impression of knowing more than one who went before and having yourself in a distancing relation to it. So, inherent in the critical act is a self-reflective act, and there is certainly, in irony, a self-reflective moment.

If one looks at it historically, the great moment as far as the theory of irony is concerned would not be contemporary, but would be Romantic irony in Germany in the early nineteenth century. If you want to go to the major texts on irony, you will not find them in contemporary writers. You would have to go back to at least the nineteenth century.

Still, it appears that there is always something self-conscious about criticism and which has some emphasis on criticism. Even when it is flourishing, criticism tends simply to be equated with irony.

I'm just saying that it is one of the tropes or one of the terms that is used more often than thirty or forty years ago.

That's especially true in the American perspective. The New Critic put the term *irony* into circulation. But in speaking of tropes, just as of metaphor, there would now be a stronger emphasis on irony, as there has been more emphasis on prose narrative than on, let's say, lyrical poetry, and from the moment you get into problems of narrative and the novel, irony is connected to narration. That emphasis is very important.

There are several techniques used to control the fictional text: one is the fiction masquerading as autobiography because it represents the greatest validity. Is the claim itself ironic? Is it too pretentious?

The claim of control, yes, when it is made, can always be shown to be unwarranted—one can show that the claim of control is a mistake, that there are elements in the text that are not controlled, that it is always possible to read the text against the overt claim of control. But irony is for me something much more fundamental than that. One gets beyond problems of self-reflection, self-consciousness. For me, irony is not something one can historically locate, because what's involved in irony is precisely the impossibility of a system of linear and coherent narrative. There is an inherent conflict or tension between irony on the one hand and history on the other, between irony on the one hand and self-consciousness on the other.

Irony comes into being precisely when self-consciousness loses its control over itself. For me, at least, the way I think of it now, irony is not a figure of self-consciousness. It's a break, an interruption, a disruption. It is a moment of loss of control, and not just for the author but for the reader as well.

Is irony temporal, essentially?

Not essentially. The proof for the fact that it is not entirely temporal or not simply temporal is that you can localize ironic moments in an effect as if they happened at one specific instant.

Do you distinguish this, then, from more conventional forms of irony, such as found in the drama or in Shakespeare?

I'm not at all comfortable with those various distinctions— dramatic irony, narrative irony. Irony, of all tropes, if it is a trope, is the most difficult, the most all-encompassing, and the hardest of all to pin down. The great ironists, and the great texts on irony are very difficult and very hard to locate. Socrates is the original *eiron,* the original ironist, and the original figure has a lot to do with relationships between philosophical and literary texts. That would be a way to answer your original question.

Yet the interest in irony at the present seems more or less to converge, or be symptomatic of, the relationship between the philosophic and literary. Anything having to do with irony includes figures like Plato, Montaigne, Schlegel, Kierkegaard, Nietzsche, who are the borderline between literature and philosophy.

Who before Nietzsche would be the main representative of this?

Friedrich Schlegel was a critic who made very high claims for criticism and also had a strong interest in philosophy because of the predominance of German idealist thought; but he was also a writer of fiction and his work is therefore very hard to locate in terms of generic distinctions. He was also a theoretician of irony.

Would you include Kierkegaard in this tradition? His first long written work was on irony.

Yes, it was his master's thesis.

Does Kierkegaard's later interest in the quest as a literary and philosophical topic add to the ironic?

The quest motif in itself is not an ironic motif. The quest is a story that has a beginning and an end, which sets its own aim, and which then proceeds, as a continuity, to an end. A quest romance, myth, story, is a linear and coherent narrative which allows us to order a variety of episodes to a totalizing principle in which the elements converge. Such a process is not incompatible with irony, but on the other hand, irony would always undo or undermine that type of narrative. So there is indeed a relationship between quest and irony, but it is itself ironic.

Why is the quest theme so pervasive in western literature, particularly since the medieval period?

Again, I would rather not use such historical terms. I would rather see them as different ways of reading. I think you can take any text and read it as if it were a quest. You will find in any text elements which are of the general questing kind. Namely, more than merely a "reward" (the "lady" of the quest), the text itself contains meaning, the attempt of its own understanding. A text is always difficult to understand, and what you seek and attempt to find is always the meaning you want to catch.

However, in every text, the questing you have succeeded in achieving is being undone. That's true in medieval texts or in contemporary ones. I'm not much given to historical categories.

Let's posit one text, not the Bible because it is too variegated, but, let's suppose, one work, a national poem which was studied and was the only text available. Hypothetically then, irony would be lessened because of the single specimen?

If there were one reading, yes.

So the ironic stance depends on multiple readings?

Yes, precisely. It's the play between the various readings that the ironic disruptions are awakening. One thinks of *The Divine Comedy,* which is a text, a canonical text. But another way to get at it is to say that irony undoes either canonical, historical patterns, or the deliberate meanings associated with a text, or the specific canonical associations made with a national literature, such as in England with the models of Milton, Spenser, or Shakespeare. It's a quest from then on to "recapture" the work.

It's that kind of myth, scheme, or sport that irony is concerned with.

True, perhaps, for such models, but why aren't the English Romantics often associated with irony?

This is partly in contrast with the Germans, because, again, in the theory of irony, the German Romantics were clearly important. So the English do not appear to be ironic, but that has to do with a misunderstanding of the term. With eighteenth-century fiction writers, the English models are fully apparent. But that too is a misunderstanding and an oversimplification of the term. Some think that the romantic stance can be schematized and constrained. But the correct answer would be to say, certainly, that there are ironic readings of Wordsworth, certainly, and of Shelley. They are not ironic in the ordinary sense. But in a deeper sense, or in a sense which is more germane to the theory of the term, the English Romantics are susceptible of ironic readings.

It's difficult to imagine an ironic reading of Wordsworth's "Lucy Poems," even with the aid of F. W. Bateson's commentary. But a poem of such high purpose as the "Intimations Ode" would not, by most readers, be seen as ironic. How is irony present in that ode?

I'm not sure that I can improvise that. I would have to preface it again by saying that an ironic reading of that type would be very hard to establish, since you would first have to follow through something already mentioned, the quest theme.

Well, there is an obviously ironic reading of Pope or Swift in the previous century. How can the nineteenth century be called "ironic," especially Wordsworth?

There is an obviously satirical edge to Swift and Pope, but irony is neither satire nor parody. To take a recent example from Wordsworth I have been thinking about, though not from the poems:

Wordsworth in the "Essay upon Epitaphs" advocates a mode of writing which he exemplifies with "gentle transitions," by means of development of no "sharp" disagreements or antitheses. Indeed the essay usually respects those prescriptions. The transitions in that essay are indeed often very gentle, very subtle, very carefully managed. The oppositions are very carefully mediated. So he seems to be entirely practicing what he preaches, but with one exception, namely when he talks about Pope. There, he loses all control whether gentle, transitional, subtle, or dialectical. Pope becomes the enemy. So the style, Wordsworth's, becomes highly antithetical, which is precisely the mode he has been arguing against. According to this commentary, to write like Pope is the worst thing one can do; Pope has demolished the faith of the English once and for all.

Wordsworth has a splendid argument to recommend and to explain that the mode he wants should be entirely different. *But* when he starts to write about Pope he does so in exactly the way he reproaches Pope for writing. At that moment, Wordsworth loses control, in a sense. At that moment, his text which had set up its own familiarity, mode, quest, its own coherence, suddenly breaks that coherence. I would call a moment like that ironic. We as readers, to the extent that we laugh or smile when we have irony, sort of have Wordsworth at that point: "There, you really go against your fixed text."

That's an ironic moment, though it's not an obviously political one because it's not particularly a moment of parody; but it's where the rhetorical mode applied in the text is not kept by the text. It's also a moment that frequently happens: at the moment you take a critical stance towards an author, you yourself repeat the gesture you reproach the author for making.

So that's a complex structure, because it's not Wordsworth self-consciously reflecting on that. He might become self-conscious of it, but that wouldn't change things very much. Some control is lost at that moment, and the reader thinks that he gains some control over Wordsworth. At that very moment the reader had better beware, because the process is being repeated whereby Wordsworth thought he was gaining control of Pope and then fell into the same stance.

So irony doesn't stop. You are always yourself described. The critic finds himself in his own attempted analysis. One could say that there are moments like that on another level in Wordsworth's own *Prelude*. There's irony when language starts to say things you didn't think it was saying, when words acquire meanings way beyond the one you think you are controlling and start saying things that go against your own quest for meaning or admitted intention. So irony is so fundamental, that, for me, it is no longer a trope. Irony is generally called a trope of tropes, but actually irony is a disruption of a continued field of tropological meaning.

So all people who write on irony try to limit its meanings and singularly fail to do so. It's uncontrollable because it is just that: it has to do with the lack of control of meaning.

But that's not what I used to say.

It has to do then with the relations of text to text, writer to text, and reader to text? Can you think of any other relations of varying meaning?

All those relationships which set up illusions of consciousness or illusions of conscious contact, or any image of mastering a text by some standard. . . .

There's an adage of scholastic philosophy that the human being is in part defined by contemplation, but can also contemplate the act of contemplation itself. In other words, there is self-awareness, in many dimensions, in the act of writing?

It has those aspects in it of self-reflection, but it is in precisely—let's call it the hyperbole of that structure—that there is no end to such juxtapositions, to the consciousness of consciousness; but it is a process, a game of infinite reflection which somehow cannot close itself off. So there is in irony, and all writers who deal with it become aware of this, a moment when a kind of dizziness develops which is threatened by many who try to define it, such as Wayne Booth. The "problem" is that an ironic text can be read ironically, and then you don't know where you are. Most commentators have in effect said, let's put an end to it, because this is madness. Yet that moment is present in all reflections on irony.

Is it the vertigo one could associate with the solipsist, or another kind of irresolution? Can you be ironic and be a solipsist?

No, because the solipsistic position, fundamentally, is reassuring. It's precisely the moment where the consciousness is invaded by something outside of it, or something that seems to be outside of it which cannot assimilate, or worse than that, which it thinks it has assimilated but which gets back at it in some other way.

But the real point is that you cannot say that this text is ironic and this text is not. Again, it would be very hard to determine that the texts which seem to be more necessarily the ones that are the most ironic, because they will always be best understood on the level of reading. There are always ironic readings possible, though just what such a reading of the Bible would be I'd prefer not to think about. Don't ask me that.

Are there, then, such things as valid texts?

There are no such things as valid texts. There should be no fundamentalists in criticism. There is no valid text because of various reasons. Neither is there a valid reading. There is no final authority. It *doesn't* mean, to get rid of one objection, that all readings are equally valid. There is no valid text, but some invalid texts are more validly invalid than others!

But that doesn't mean that anything goes, that you can say anything about reading. There is a considerable rigor in the way in which that statement can be made. It means that any reading of a text can be put in question, "ironized," if you wish, by another reading. This has to do with the figurality of language to the extent that figuration is not resolvable or doesn't lead to a simple pattern of meaning.

I asked about the temporal possibility of irony because of multiple consciousness in time. Isn't that also an aspect of what we've been discussing?

Texts in time can be structured, and can be categorically understood. So the temporal is assimilated into other modes of consciousness. So when we say there are no valid texts, it means that no text can be exhausted, or saturated, or fully understood in terms of its own temporal category. There will be temporal or spatial aspects of a text; they will readily be apparent in a text, but they will not saturate.

Your readings will always be overdetermined in the sense that you will end up with several more or less incompatible readings, or underdetermined in the sense that you don't even come near to what the meaning seems to be. So you are never quite there. Whether you put that temporally or in terms of the experience of the consciousness, the difficulties are inherent—I hesitate to call it in nature, but in the fact that the text is in many ways not an entity, not something that as such can be hypostasized.

There's a fairly well-known problem in the writing of Augustine, who concludes his Confessions *with a treatise on time, remarkable in part, because he admits there is no solution to the questions raised. For a solution, he therefore simply throws himself on the idea of totality in the "divine." Is your intention to take the "divine" out of reading?*

Yes, I intend to take the divine out of reading. The experience of the divine is one that is totally conceivable, but which I don't think is compatible with reading. One of the best theoreticians of irony, Friedrich Schlegel, after having said about irony some of the most astute things that anybody has ever said about it, including Kierkegaard, and, I guess, Plato to some extent, did indeed go over to a certain mode of belief and adopted a religious life. He did not after that continue as a reader. The things he then still wrote which have to do with reading don't compare with what he did before.

Generally, the act of faith is not an act of reading, or for me is not compatible with reading.

You're refuting a long tradition of one kind of reading?

Not really. The vision of reading has always had its problem with creeds. The traditional battle in the history of reading is between hermeneutics on the one hand, which is the interpretation of meaning, and rhetoric on the other hand.

The hermeneutic would pursue the single, the unified, and the rhetorical would celebrate the varied and multiple?

That would certainly be one way of putting it. Rhetoric as I understand it, for which irony is the concept of limit, is not only multiple. The multiple is also totalized—it's the disruption of the single.

Would you say something about the dogmatic approach to texts, that is, the attempted establishment of single meanings? This has been a consistent attempt in every history of interpretation, or reading, has it not?

The attempt to control is characteristic of all fundamentally theological modes of reading. There is indeed something in texts which is undecided, generally threatened, and one would see that a threat exists, that there is a considerable need for setting up canonical defenses. So you could take this as a defensive reaction.

But that's a subjective way to answer this very pertinent question. We should not merely say that texts are multiple or texts undo their unity, and so on. This is a part of a process that is at least two-faced; because if it is true that texts always undo readings, it is equally true that texts constitute meanings. So the real theoretical question is what it is in language that necessarily produces meanings but that also undoes what it produces. That question would lead one either to speculations on the nature of language, or to questions about the philosophy or epistemology of language which would assume tropes and something else that is not tropes—and this would lead to speculations on the nature of language.

But if the question is asked like this—Why a given reaction at a specific time?—the discussion can always be put in historical terms.

Therefore, I like the idea of the quest for meaning, because it is inherent in any text or language. So the position I'm holding is not one of radical skepticism, or one like it. As a matter of fact, with any text it is interesting to see the immense elasticity of the hermeneutic pressure, the immense ability the mind has to set up meanings and to try to outwit any undoing of meaning.

On the other hand, there is between those two tendencies an irresolvable conflict. Pascal, who is good on that, will look at the history of philosophy as an opposition between what he calls the *dogmatic* and the *skeptical*. That irreconcilable battle which one tries to reduce to a dialectical opposition of tensions which could possibly be resolved is not, for Pascal, resolved.

In other words, commentary in all its forms, Biblical exegesis, criticism, explanation, is illusory?

Yes, that is illusory at all times, and patterns of totalization are. . . .

Always open to correction?

Worse than correction, demolition.

So the process of criticism is itself, and this word, with aporia, *frequently appears in criticism recently, is itself oxymoronic, and you were of course aware of this in titling your book* Blindness and Insight?

Darkness and the relation to the sun, dark and light, always come up in those patterns. Surely, poetic texts thrive on tropes of that type, that kind of binary opposition. It's very—it can always be shown that that runs to a set program of statement, or emphasis. That's not wrong, but what's naive, or a simplification of patterns, is that they are symmetrical—white, black, and so on—so they work like binary oppositions. An attentive reading can show that those simple oppositions are not operative at the really crucial moments in the text.

Aporia, which you mentioned, is no longer an oxymoron, because in *aporia* you have a truly logical conflict, a true opposition which blocks. This is not true of oxymoron, which goes on continually and can keep going on and engendering texts.

At least one source, however, gives aporia *a much more polite definition that can be related to praeterition, mainly a rhetorical device or strategy.*

I would see it, rather, as an impasse which cannot be resolved, domesticated, or assimilated by a trope. Tropes are most amazing in putting together the most incongruous, incompatible things, but there are certain points where the trope cannot master the disruption. The history of the term is complicated. Therefore I don't know if it is that useful.

It's remarkable that you go back to rhetorical terms and revive a terminology thought antiquated. While there was a revival in the

Midwest about twenty years ago of "rhetoric," and a revival of the
terminology that reached even into a very few college writing texts,
the tradition and its language were thought dead. No one at all, even
the Chicago Aristotelians, generally used these rhetorical terms. Yet
you seize the terms and shake them into life though many assume
that rhetorical terminology is moribund. Why have you used it?

I have by no means always used that terminology. It is not at
all present in *Blindness and Insight,* for instance. I come, in my own
education, from a kind of existential philosophical mode of discourse that was used on the continent by critics like Blanchot or
philosophers like Heidegger, and while all people speak about language, they usually do so either in an ontological language or the
language of the subject, the language of the self. That's the mode
in which I was brought up.

Then in this country I was exposed to a new kind of reading,
a much closer mode of reading, basically a New Critical mode of
reading. I had always had an attraction for, and was interested in,
the writings of the French critics in the moment of close reading
that seemed to raise certain problems that they were not expressing
all too successfully.

Blanchot, Sartre?

Yes, Blanchot, Sartre, Bachelard, also Heidegger, Hegel—a language of consciousness of temporality, a language with some phenomenological overtones. But I've always been interested in the
categories that would be more linguistic. So I found great interest
in the New Critics who were clearly more responsive to structures
that were more linguistic, even though they did not use too much
of the terminology that had to do with rhetoric, and even though
they were interested in organic form, totalities of meaning, and so
forth, interests which I didn't necessarily share. So I can't say when
or how, but certainly not under the influence of the Chicago Aristotelians. But I had great relief in finding terminology that had something to do with tropes, by thinking about the relation between
allegory and symbolism.

But incidentally, with structural linguistics, with Jakobson and
people whom I had known at Harvard, that vocabulary became

much more visible, though even with the so-called structuralists, the problem of rhetoric was never dominant. But at any rate, some of those terms were put more in circulation. One could not just say *metaphor* or *symbol* or *image*.

But then it was really to some extent an eye opener, first of all, to see how much in philosophy had already been said about it; but the main revelation for me was Nietzsche, whom I had been trying to read for many years without getting too far, precisely because the moment where Nietzsche reflects on language as a historical structure is a moment which one didn't know or didn't hear about. One was so concerned with problems of good and evil, problems of an ethical nature, or historical attitudes, much of which I couldn't get into. But Nietzsche is highly aware of rhetorical theory, knows those terms and uses them. It gives you a point of entry that is exceedingly fruitful.

Nietzsche provided you with this terminology?

No, I found it to be operative in Nietzsche. I found it in the New Criticism, certainly, and through the discipline of close reading. Because when you start to read closely you find that you cannot gloss the linguistic structures which you can account for only by means of tropes. Not that those are "complete"—I don't believe in them as a taxonomy but as a transformational system. However, I found the terms require a kind of attention to texts: [the reader is required] to look for those structures for which the tropes are the kind of reversals involved in metalepsis, the kind of totalization involved in synecdoche, the kind of interruptions involved in aposiopesis.

But this was quickly rationalized or schematized in a simple binary system, metaphor-metonymy. Jakobson went so far as to call it poetry-prose, or paradigmatic-syntagmatic. That attempt to master a system of tropes by reducing it to an actual system is itself a typical tropological fallacy, though it has provided for valid readings which can be shown, very specifically at certain points, to be false to the extent that there are elements in texts which cannot be accounted for by that system. It can account for certain elements in texts, but it has to ignore others.

Do you think that metonymy and metaphor are a kind of misreading? Of course, that word [metaphor] has loomed, or bloomed, large in The Map of Misreading, *where it is called* misprision. *Isn't metaphor, and the whole apparatus of tropes, a species of misreading?*

I don't so much speak of misreading, because misreading supposes a right reading. It's a mouthful and it's not felicitous, but I speak of unreadability, which means that the text produces not misreadings, but readings that are incompatible. So you can, from a text, deduce a reading which is perfectly consistent with figuration that's active in the text, but you can also deduce another reading which is semantically incompatible with the first. The two readings, to the extent that they can be reduced to statements that are not only incompatible but which undo each other, conflict radically.

In that sense, you can say that a text is unreadable—going back to the beginning of our conversation, the fact that there is no single reading. So I don't see so much a misreading as unreadability.

You said before that there's no validity of reading, but that does not mean that "anything goes." Now, what establishes a greater or lesser validity, or at the least, a greater or lesser estimate of process?

Certainly some kind of form of rigor; and again, the basis for that is tropological. Tropes have a consistency: tropological movements are not wild. They are systematic, or *systemic,* one would say—that is, they engender systems. As such, they have consistency, and their power as well as their seduction is in their coherence. One would expect readers to be sensitive to them. That's what I would call the rigor of reading.

The interesting point is that there may be two rigorous readings which are demonstrably disciplined, attentive, responsive to nuances, yet are incompatible, or lead to conflicts, or lead to unresolvable cruxes that one has then to face as steps. So in that sense, although one could say that there is no valid reading as such, nevertheless readings can never be rigorous enough and demand their own rigor. So it's not that they should be given merely subjective, or, in the bad sense of the term, impressionist reactions.

Are texts, or readings, inherently metaleptic?

Metaleptic in the sense that they take cause for effect, that they reverse the normal order in which the text precedes the reading?

Yes.

Surely there's a priority of the author before the critic, but that's a false model. Within the text itself it's impossible to separate moments of writing from moments of reading in the text, so that it is always possible within the text itself to reverse those priorities. An author doesn't invent something and then start to read it. Any invention is always already a reading, and any reading is an invention, to some extent.

That's often completely misunderstood, and people say, "Those critics, nowadays, want to equate reading with writing because they would really like to be writers." That's really not the point at all. The humility of the critic in relation to the work is total, and there is no attempt to get ahead of it or equate one order of writing with another. If that were true, it would lead to absolutely inane criticism.

Something more complicated is being said. When you write the text you are constantly reading. Anyone who writes a text is at that moment reading it, and the production of a text is as much an act of reading as it is writing. As a matter of fact, that opposition is not tenable but gets simply transported to the writer on the one hand and the critical reader on the other. There is a battle for power between both, a sort of naive allegory.

This has a great deal to do with other patterns of opposition in western culture, such as soul and body, or in Descartes, body and mind?

Those binary models keep coming up. That's the trope, that's the metaphor of the binary. It sets up the substitution of resemblance, and resemblances are very easily put into antithetical concepts. Metaphor itself generates such polarizations.

You have been working with concepts of metaphor and theories of language in your work on Rousseau, and you have written a book on the subject. What's the title?

It's called *Allegories of Reading*. It deals mostly with Rousseau, but also deals with Nietzsche and Proust, while it continues the argument about Rousseau.

Do you deal with the confusions of Rousseau's literary personae?

No, the confusions of the literary traditions he engendered.

You were not interested, then, in Irving Babbitt's attack, or others based on moralistic grounds, on the "deceptiveness" of Rousseau?

No. I was interested, however, in the curiously perplexing and on the other hand quite outrageous tradition of Rousseau-reading. Rousseau is one of the authors who is read totally aberrantly, so that the commonplaces of literary and intellectual history associated with Rousseau are particularly remote from the text, especially in the traditional criticism.

What are the chief commonplaces?

The oldest is the one that deemed Rousseau to be a writer of "nature," "primitive nature," or "back to nature," or thought of him as having advocated a "state of nature." It started as soon as the *First Discourse* came out, and very soon after that Rousseau wrote a strong protest against it. Surely there was something to it; he was in a sense calling for it, and one can't say that he was entirely innocent.

Certainly another and much more subtle reading is Rousseau as the "author of the self." But that is also quite inadequate in dealing with some aspects of the subject. I have no special sympathy for Rousseau. That's not it, but it's a very interesting canon. It's thematically so diversified, between its political aspects, its professional aspects, and the fictional, novelistic aspects that it's a challenge to find—I don't want to call it a unifying principle because it turns out to be a principle that is not unified—but at least to find some kind of language which allows you to circulate without falling into any traps of very simplified opposition, either political or aesthetic, "confessional" or "objective."

I would like to ask you about the title of your earlier essay "Theory of Metaphor in Rousseau's Second Discourse*" in* Romanticism: Vistas, Instances, Continuities. *Seeing this title one might ask, why* metaphor *in Rousseau—isn't that an astounding title?*

I guess so. By now I am so used to it that I don't find the association unusual. However, true, it's not Rousseau-nature, Rousseau-confession, and so forth, but there had been awareness in some of the commentators, Starobinski for instance, that Rousseau was very concerned with theory of language. The eighteenth century was very involved with such theory. One knew that, but those texts were considered more or less secondary. Rousseau's essay on the origin of language was considered a very minor text, but had not been totally ignored. So when I used that title it was not so paradoxical.

I would like to ask you to comment on two passages from the essay. The first is, "Rousseau seems to want to have it both ways, giving himself the freedom of the fabulator but, at the same time, the authority of the responsible historian." Are you saying that he thought history was more reliable than fiction?

No, certainly not. In that piece I'm not saying how that is with Rousseau. I'm saying that's what historians say about Rousseau. So this is not my argument. However, it is a frequent and legitimate complaint one can make about Rousseau, specifically in reference to the *Second Discourse* where he says we must do away with all facts, and instead of facts start out with a pure fiction, which is the state of nature, not a historical fact but a pure fiction, as such. That creates an immediate methodological problem, which is what I speak about in the passage cited because how can [Rousseau] have a text that claims to be historical and that claims to be talking about the actual structure of society as it exists for him at that time? You can only understand the political structure of society by resorting to pure fiction, a state of nature, but you have to posit this fiction in order to understand. So historians will say, what is this historian doing demanding fiction, and literary people will say, what is this fabulator doing talking about history?

That's a good thing, but the crux, the difficulty, the trouble which halts the interpretation of Rousseau is the claim that you can understand what seems to be this methodological operation as a methodological insanity, which is then often explained by referring to the pathology of Rousseau, some of his own confessional statements about it. A critic may say, you know, that reality is something so unbearable that he had to invent all kinds of fictions and had to people the world with the creatures of his imagination because he couldn't confront a reality which is not very interesting.

However, you can really understand what's at play only if you understand Rousseau's concept of language, very specifically his notion of metaphor. Because then, when you see that it is in the nature of all discourse at all times to have its necessarily fictional component as a consequence of a linguistic domain, and [when you see that this component] is present in all discourse and especially genetic discourse of this type, you don't resort to biographical fantasy.

So, true, Rousseau *seems* to want to have it both ways, but there is in his concept of language an element that accounts for that necessity.

You conclude the paragraph that contains the comment about the fabulator and the historian with this: "How can a pure fiction and a narrative involving such concrete political realities as property, contractual law, and modes of government coalesce into a genetic history that pretends to lay bare the foundation of human society?" You say that that is accomplished through metaphor, in part?

Right. It is by taking into account the element in Rousseau which is curiously and systematically ignored, namely, his underlying theory of metaphor. I tried to show specifically that, at the crucial moment, theory comes into the foreground, and also how, in the tradition of viewing Rousseau, those moments are refused or put aside.

So the critical stereotype is that a writer is either a literal historian or a speculator, one or the other?

That runs true through the history of Rousseau interpretation. Either he is much too literally a historian or he is just totally mad, or totally private.

As you are describing this, I am reminded of a good deal of criticism of the Romantics, even of Shelley.

Yes, he is similar in his critics' eyes in many ways. He is viewed either as a vegetarian madman or a fanatical political activist who had no respect for historical or political continuity.

One can generalize this and say that is the way Romanticism is seen. That's still the general diagnosis. Romanticism is both irrational and, on the other hand, curiously literal-minded in its own political praxis.

The other quotation I want to ask you about is this: "The impossibility of reaching a rationally enlightened anthropology also accounts for the necessary leap into fiction, since no past or present human action can coincide with or be underway toward the nature of man." If one "leaps into fiction," that means there's reality somewhere doesn't it?

I guess the key notion that this depends on is man. Rousseau in the *Second Discourse* starts to become a historian, and tells us about the history of mankind, and how mankind came to be in a deplorable condition. Of course, one can always agree that the condition of the present is deplorable—that is always the case!

Now the curious thing in what he says is that for Rousseau the notion *man* is undefinable, and this is very much, again, in a tradition which includes Pascal, who also says that *man* is always beyond man. Nietzsche's *man* constantly transcends himself, which you can put in theological terms, if you wish. That's not the way Rousseau puts it, but in its own way, that is how the *Second Discourse* starts. It is impossible for man to define himself as an entity with specific links. Therefore, the anthropology, or science, or entity which is undefinable cannot be simply a history.

You can write a history, well, of the city of New Haven, which is a legal concept, more or less definable geographically. You can say that would be possible. That is a legitimate signature or entity. But *man* is never a proper name—it is for me, since I am called de Man, but *man*, in the sense of *mankind,* cannot be accurately generalized to include the variety of human life.

Again, Rousseau will say that writing is in a tradition that is very well established. There is no entity that can be defined as man. Therefore, there is necessarily in the history of this undefinable entity, *man,* an undefinable, fictional, fantastic element.

In some ways, that's even Christian!

Sartre in Nausea *develops such a theme with care in the characterization of Roquentin, a would-be historian who can never gather enough material about Rollebon, a courtier-opportunist at the court of Louis* XVIII. *On the other hand, Roquentin visits the official gallery of his own town and reads the official histories of the men in the portraits. He finds most of the accounts are falsified—so the perplexity remains for a much more nearly contemporaneous group. These themes are very much a part of the twentieth century?*

That would be a very Rousseauistic moment in Sartre, certainly. Rousseau says, much more radically, that we must begin by forgetting all the facts. That's a sound historical instinct.

Is Hayden White's Metahistory . . .

Yes, Hayden White reads Rousseau well, and can see history as tropology. Hayden White is a contemporary Rousseauist!

Doesn't Descartes's First Meditation *have a good deal of interplay between doubt and assertion?*

I've recently been interested in Descartes and Rousseau, and it's very possible to show, not the same problems but problems of the same type as those which are so glaring in Rousseau, or anyway are in somewhat the same tradition and occur there too. Though the argument is entirely different, it requires in both cases that you go back to theories of language. It is very interesting, as a recurrence, that in the history of interpretations linguistic theory is always dodged. In a way, it makes one suspicious of that theory which people would rather not know about. That [suspicion] so deeply inhabits the tradition that you do not necessarily come upon the true Descartes in the *Meditations.*

Isn't this history of skepticism especially strong in France?

This is always said to be French. It's one of the ways of dealing with the problem, by saying, "Oh, it's French." So you can then claim that it is not very serious. By doing that it's made kind of harmless. But there are very English versions of that which are overlooked, in Locke and Shelley, for instance. One can take the other tack for German writing by saying Germans are incapable of irony; all is lost in pathos.

There is a French version of skepticism, certainly. Descartes is very French. Even though he wrote in Latin, the skepticism is apparent!

So the problem is not tied to a specific nationality.

What is meant by the "epistemology of metaphor"?

I think it's a false distinction to say that literary texts are aesthetic and therefore do not raise epistemological questions, whereas philosophical texts are scientific and address epistemological questions. That distinction doesn't hold. Aesthetic is not independent of epistemology. If there is a priority, that is if there has to be one, it certainly is epistemological. Any reading must include it. Certain decisions about truth and falsehood or certain presuppositions about truth and falsehood—that is, about the possibility of meaning—are epistemological.

Don't you bring Kant into this discussion as a "modern" in the stating of epistemological and aesthetic problems?

In "Epistemology of Metaphor" there is a little section on Kant, and people who read Kant do not like that section. I discuss his treatment of metaphor, the use of illustrative, sensory passages to describe abstractions, the use of hypotyposis.

Kant is very important, and I think that whatever I tried to do with Rousseau one could do with Kant. As a matter of fact, Kant is constantly on my mind in Rousseau. Kant had considerable admiration for Rousseau and read him much better than most people do. I think that Kant is also very misread, and that one of the forms of misreading Kant has to do with the simplification of the notion of the aesthetic. Nonetheless, the *Critique* should be reread and reinterpreted.

Does he avoid the dualism you have spoken about by his emphasis on the noumena? *Kant appears precisely not to be epistemological, seems to be attempting to leap over, to escape, earlier epistemological definitions, particularly skeptical ones?*

Kant is a critical philosopher and a philosopher of limitations, and that is a very epistemological enterprise. So the critique of Kant in Fichte and Hegel tries to move away from a mere philosophy of limitations, boundaries, or prudence.

So this is part of your interest in the changing of boundaries through rereadings?

Yes. The tradition of readings of Kant is a good example of a rich tradition in which very diversified and incompatible elements come together. All the way up to Heidegger, Kant remains absolutely central. My main interest in the problem of reading in relation to Kant is that critics have read his aesthetic as a closing category, as a limitation for epistemological inquiry. That's a way in which Kant still is used in a certain aestheticism, to degrees toward which I have a very polemical relationship. Because if you see in an epistemological relationship something dangerous, or in irony something dangerous—to go back to our starting point—very often the aesthetic is invoked to hold that "danger" within boundaries. Very often, Kant is invoked as the authority for that particular strategy. If there is something in irony that is vertiginous but viewed as an "aesthetic effect," it is not really "dangerous." However, a careful rereading of Kant's aesthetics would make the use of this stratagem much more suspicious.

How would you define the term deconstruction*?*

It's possible, within a text, to frame a question or to undo assertions, made in the text by means of elements which are in the text, which frequently would be precisely structures that play off rhetorical against grammatical elements.

The term deconstruction *has a slightly negative connotation.*

It is double-faced. *Construction* is inherent in the term *deconstruction,* but deconstruction is not demolition.

But one is not able to speak of creation *and* un- *or* de-creation*. The problem with the term* deconstruction *is that it at first appears not to be creative, which is one of the supposed functions of the process of its view of reading.*

Derrida used the term and put it on the map. Now it's become a war cry. That's too bad, because in a sense the term is no longer really useful. It's a mere label. Precisely the question about whether it's a positive or negative process is the question which should not be asked, or should not primarily be asked. There is a negative moment in it, as there is a negative moment in any critical reading that is not simply, shall we say, nihilistic. I don't want to be too sanguine about this. However, we are doing something positive.

I think the opposition of positive-negative as far as reading is concerned, or as far as certain historical valorizations are concerned, is just the binary opposition one would want to deconstruct. So if "deconstruct" is an effective way of questioning positive and negative valorizations, that's good.

Is it androgynous?

Well, it doesn't attempt to deconstruct male-female oppositions! It just says it is a form of division. So it's androgynous if you want, yes. But it's not totalizing.

Deconstruction asserts simultaneity?

It's simultaneous asymmetry.

The trouble with the term, perhaps, is its implicit assertion of temporality, of definite time patterns. Texts are constructed, then deconstructed?

Once you're sensitized to it, it's a metaphor that frequently appears, especially in a positive form, in architechtonic structures. To think of a text as a structure or a construction is against this somewhat naive notion of structuralism that assumed it could describe structures as synchronic systems. Though I don't really know if Derrida invented the term, I certainly first saw it in his writing in *Grammatology*—so it very much coincides with structuralism, the idea of texts as grids, as patterns. So it's in that polemical context.

There is writing about architectural modernism that comments on theories of positive and negative space and very consciously designed mathematical relationships of grids and proportions within grids.

Deconstruction is such a textual notion. There is a spatial metaphor when construction-deconstruction is mentioned.

Yet the relation is coincidental?

I think so.

I would like, finally, to ask you about Derrida's use of Freud, his reading of Freud, whom he not only rereads but uses in new ways of interpretation. Is this in part what you have been asserting about the generation of texts, of their power? Derrida addresses Freud as a text rather than as a psychoanalytic, medical scripture. This has created many different readings, among them the subject of irresolution, and levels of discontinuity. Why wasn't it recognized before that there were such topics in Freud?

No doubt, Derrida changed the emphasis. He's not the only one. Lacan did similar things, and the two enterprises are entirely separable, though there are many, many points of dissent between them. First of all, in both cases, for Lacan and Derrida, Freud had first to be read, therefore had to be treated as a text and read as such. That's very different from canonical readings, which assume Freud to be an established scientific certitude which has to be taken as such. Even if they admitted some of Freud's philosophical speculations, or his speculations on culture, religion, and so on, and separated them from the clinical element, the readings might still be canonical. So it makes a difference, not only in the reading itself, but where you put the emphasis.

But the test would be whether Freud were really unavoidable, or, even, perhaps, uncontrollable. No critical text, really, no theory of text, according to Derrida, can come into being if it avoids Freud.

So there's a certain scandal that is accomplished?

I'm not so sure. Whatever one would be saying about texts or a series of texts by use of rhetorical, and to some extent philosophical terminology, would necessarily fall short of valid critical commentary. I think that what was performed for Lacan, Derrida, and others by Freud was done for me by Heidegger.

However, doesn't Freud specifically write about the relation of the cryptic and the public, the hidden and the open, the different kinds of concealing that you write about critically?

What was performed for Lacan, Derrida, and others by Freud was done for me by Heidegger and those in his tradition—Hegel and Kant—and includes a way of reading, and [a way of] reading philosophical texts, and a way of putting philosophical texts in relation to poetic and literary texts.

What are Heidegger's own "revealing" and "hiding" metaphors?

Heidegger himself was very suspicious of metaphor, because his theory of language does not allow for the play of differences and the play of misleading elements that are involved in the pattern of metaphor. I think he sees unmediated revelations of language. However, by speaking of them as revelations and by speaking of truth as *Realität* (which he sees in *Holzwege* as destroying of the veil), he places you very much in that metaphorical system of hiding and revealing. Heidegger is engaged in attempting to account for certain recurrent operations in the repeated, interpretive gestures of cognition. His tropes are not so different from some of the fundamental tropes used by Freud, although there is a very constant avoidance of Freud in Heidegger's discourse.

When I say that Heidegger can play for me the role that Freud plays for Derrida, that makes some sense in terms of both their predominant metaphors. . . .

READINGS

A bibliography of Paul de Man's work appears in the memorial issue, "The Lesson of Paul de Man," *Yale French Studies* 69 (1985). *Blindness and Insight* (Oxford University Press, 1971) was reissued in a new edition with additional essays (University of Minnesota Press, 1983). The same press is to publish or has published *The Resistance to Theory, Aesthetic Ideology* (1986), and *Fugitive Essays,* edited respectively by Wlad Godzich, Andrzej Warminski, and Lindsay Waters. *The Rhetoric of Romanticism* (Columbia University Press) was issued in 1984. *Blindness and Insight, Allegories of Reading* (Yale University Press, 1979), and the translation and edition of Flaubert's *Madame Bovary* (W. W. Norton, 1965) are the only books by de Man not to appear posthumously.

CODA:
VIEWCOUNTERVIEW

So you have finished with your interviews?

Well, some would say that the interview is an unending form. However, yes, for the time being, they are finished. Yet in a way an interview is like a successful conversation. One doesn't want it to end.

What's the historical precedent for the interview?

Well, there are immediate precedents for the form, for instance the *Paris Review* series on "authors," that strange term in English which excludes writers of criticism. But I didn't have those in mind when I started this project. The "interviews" which are most in memory are those dialogues which Robert Craft conducted either with himself or with Stravinsky in the pages of the *New York Review of Books* in the late 1960s or early '70s. They compose some of the wittiest things said about any art, no matter who said or wrote what, no matter what the circumstances of composition or the coincidence of "reality."

Craft could hardly be said to be nonpartisan or a "critic" of Stravinsky. Have you also partly invented or embellished the answers to your questions? Are you also a partisan?

The participants in this venture saw the typescripts of the finished interviews and made a few corrections. But of course I am not a partisan of any of the critics interviewed, and I trust that my basic skepticism about all matters literary and critical is apparent. For me, the history of criticism is a record of misunderstandings and of succeeding hypotheses which work for a while and are then discarded, but remain, like the junked cars parked outside some upstate New York farmhouses, as a kind of presence, useless but intrusively memorable. Yet there are several hundreds of English and American academicians still riding in the flivver of Aristotelianism, archaic but restored, and they still recite the catalog of Aristotelian parts avidly and with total belief, Klaxon, magneto, peripety, anagnoresis. I got a good dose of this indirectly from studying at a Jesuit college where several courses in the Schoolman Aquinas were then required for every undergraduate—the good old days! So Aristotelian terms still form a kind of indelible subconsciousness. Most emphatically, though, I do not chant these terms as though they were the magic phrases which unlock the meaning of language and literary experience, and neither do any of the victims of these interviews. None of them is involved in the restoration of old historical documents of criticism. Even Geoffrey Hartman, who is more and more taken with the Jewish Bible and commentary, doesn't utter words and phrases from the "classics" as though they were permanent or eternal sayings of the fathers. Well, maybe he does, but the information is for a non-Jew so novel and arresting that he doesn't seem to be merely polishing the same old phrases year after year. So, no, obviously, I am *not* a partisan.

How did you come to this group of critics?

I had read just a little of Bloom's work before having his National Endowment for the Humanities seminar at Yale in the 1970s. One reading led to another. I was extremely doubtful about Bloom's entire enterprise during and after that experience, but what finally convinced me of the validity of his intentions were the negative and petty comments that always accompany the mention of the "Yale critics," "gang of four," or whatever. A good deal of nonsensical, absurd, and even vicious gossip also exists about the group. For a while I was nonplussed: the level of discussion in faculty committee meetings *is* the level of discussion about academic matters in print! In other words, the sentences and phrases most memorable for their stupidity and awkwardness in one's day-to-day academic experiences are also printed in kind. Humanities professors in general and (as they are called in the U.S.) English professors in particular think of themselves as carrying on not merely a discipline, but a kind of moral code, much like the pathological gossips in any community. There is also the problem of academic pride, impossible to discuss, really, except that the writers of squibs against this group, no matter how uninformed, think themselves in higher estimation because of their extrovert sins of illogic and bias.

Still, I am not a partisan of the Yale group. They are just more interesting and productive than most academicians now writing on literature. That doesn't mean, however, that I read them or anyone else for "truth."

You don't agree with Harold Bloom, then?

I agree with all of the four in the sense that they force an inquiring reader to look again at texts more closely and more energetically: they force a reader to compare *that* text, *those* texts, with others. A lot of commentary on this group says that they are related to the New Critics, Cleanth Brooks, Inc. His and "Red" Warren's and other New Critics' hypothesis was the autonomous text, the fiction that a text may be examined by itself isolated from its fellows. This is still a good antidote to historicism, but is far too narrow a basis for reading. Anyone above the level of informational reading, the scanner of recipes, medicine bottles, cereal boxes and textbooks, knows that reading takes place on a much more complex level, and that all texts are related to others. With their differing vocabularies and approaches, all four of this Yale group see texts in this manner, not as autonomous and isolated. There is a somewhat fundamentalist and Protestant strain in both Brooks and Warren. Still, it's a good introduction to other forms of reading, but not *the* reading. No one has the final reading, of course.

But to what extent do you agree with Bloom and the others?

I don't see how anyone can effectively deny the basic tenets of what Bloom sets forth in *The Anxiety of Influence.* Of course that work is far from being a primer. The terminology is odd, probably intentionally to avoid the repetition of other critical terms, and the language of the book is itself heavy, baroque, convoluted. However, not only are the statements there valid about literature, they are useful in the other arts as well. Every great artist at first quotes from a predecessor and then breaks away into a strong and personally realized "language." J. S. Bach's quotation of Vivaldi, Chopin of Bellini and John Field, Schubert of Voricek, Brahms of Schumann, Stravinsky of Rimsky-Korsakov, Whistler of Watteau, Picasso of Braque, just where does the process end? However, I do find the models which Bloom uses for this process at times disconcerting. For the most part, he ignores Spenser and even Shakespeare, the two most commanding figures in British literature, and replaces them with Milton. Bloom also hasn't accounted for the creator's reliance on an inferior model, Keats on Tom Moore, for instance. Nonetheless, the consistent restatement and the refinement of Bloom's theories have been convincing. He has been advocating this theory with increasing conviction and success just about since I first met him some fifteen years ago. Also, his critics have helped. For the most part they are hopeless misreaders of a primary kind of simplicity.

Did anything surprise you in the interviews?

I did expect the subjects to be more passionate and forensic in their reactions to their negative critics. For the most part, they simply turned aside from negative comments, which I read to them, and refused to engage in argument. Bloom was the exception here, and is one of the most redoubtable of arguers. He skewers Cynthia Ozick yet again in this last interview done in the fall of 1985, and his remarks about the literary journalists Epstein, Kramer, and Podhoretz (whom he at one point calls Podhorrors), are hilarious and devastating. Bloom must be one of the most formidable opponents in language now living. He could even survive in that bull pit of terms and tenets, the British Parliament.

Doesn't this violate the decorum of criticism?

Of course. But the attackers violated it first, and "decorum" is used by academicians to cover a multitude of scabs and running clauses of abuse—all kinds of verbal sin.

Again, this sounds partisan.

No, no. I am merely describing what's been going on in the reviews.

Don't you use these writers in your own teaching?

Just for the first time in the last year. However, I started with the modern and deconstructionist methods and worked back to Aristotle's *Poetics*. It somewhat reminds me of the reading of Horace I did as a college youngster. It seemed very mild and old hat. A few years later I read a lot of Swinburne, then just happened to pick up Horace. Believe me, Horace has never seemed to be such *a major writer*. The misleading simplicities of Aristotle were just as refreshing!

You are not yourself a deconstructionist?

Even though the critical results are at times fascinating, I find the terminology oppressive and precious. I came to Derrida after reading a lot of French existentialism, and I find even with his published denials, Derrida's consistent ahistoricism just too coy and artificial a stance, somewhat like a nudist taking pride in his extrovert bareness on a solitary beach outside all sight save his own. Oddly enough, I find the translations of Derrida by the disciple de Man more refreshing than the "master" himself. Of course, Derrida has been partly stitched with a kind of fig-leafing by his less able disciples who revel in the vocabulary for its own sake and do the usual imitative clipping and pasting of categories and rough stitching of pages. On the other hand, as Hillis Miller observes, what Derrida himself says about particular texts can be illuminating, at times even burning in intensity. Generally, however, to continue with the nudist metaphor, the imitators of Derrida have usually been more burned than warmed on the sandy beaches.

What do you think is most valuable in this collection?

Of course, I am not going to value any remark above any other in this collection. Nonetheless I have fantasized that Paul de Man's statement about irony could be forged, hammered into wrought iron, and made into an entry to the Yale campus: "There is no valid text, but some texts are more validly invalid than others!" If only in some future state this could replace the well-wrought slogan, "For God, Country, and Yale." Is that the right sequence?

I don't know.

The other surprising issue that came out of these interviews is the difference between Geoffrey Hartman and Harold Bloom on the matter of Jewish Studies. The remarks are not antagonistic. They are antiphonal, also in different keys, yes, major and minor.

With which do you agree?

Well, I'm a nonbeliever. I can't say more than that. Just compare the texts and make up your own mind.

So far you have said little about Geoffrey Hartman.

That's more of a statement than a question! However, Hartman is opening a new form of historical and experiential discourse related to the Holocaust and the act of being a Jew, the outsider at high levels of academe who is strong enough to take energy from his "difference." Any academician worth his footnotes should take courage from this stance. Learning is an alien occupation these days and perhaps always has been since the decline of state religions. But such remarks only lead to differences with those interviewed, so I have no more to say at present.

What of a personal nature have you omitted from the interviews?

Well, all mention of the conditions of the interviews themselves. Perhaps metaphorically, one was conducted to the running of a vacuum cleaner in another room. That made for an interesting tape recording! "Would you . . . 'OOm—OOm.'" For a few instances during the transcription to type, I thought that I had somehow gotten lost in an early 1970s live performance by the author of *Howl*, who at that time invoked one of the monosyllables of that which "surpasseth all understanding" and accompanied himself with an autoharp. I couldn't hear any autoharp so was saved from aural and cultural vertigo! Also I hadn't read Allen Ginsberg for a while, so that was of some aid.

Are you being serious? What have you left out of the interviews? The roar of that vacuum cleaner?

There was a good deal said off the tape either before or after the interviews themselves that should find some note. I urged Geoffrey Hartman to write of his experiences when he fled Germany to England in the 1930s. Even though being in England saved his life, his experiences while there are Dickensian in the dark senses of that term.

There is also the matter of Bloom and Hartman being hired at Yale at the same time in the 1950s and being put in a basement office by the old Yankee overseers, now supposedly long gone. The office walls were crawling with silverfish—probably an old Populist reaction to Yale's economic conservatism and the adherence to the gold standard by William Howard Taft, but not understood by the new and still relatively innocent instructors as an entomological irony.

I've learned that you wrote a serious introduction to these interviews, complete with footnotes.

Quite so, but it is permanently discarded, if an academician ever completely discards anything. Part of the introduction was a recitation of the forensic wars of commentators and surcommentators, rebuttal and surrebuttal and counterstatement, all tedious and hopelessly repetitive. Much of this stuff, like religious apologetics and controversy, is truly bathetic: artificially deep, dark, and life-killing.

So I decided not to use the material. Besides, some of the controversies are in the interviews. I took care to quote them, whatever the effects or the responses of those questioned might be.

During this discussion, you have slighted Hillis Miller. Anything to say about him?

Though Hillis Miller is now a professor at the University of California at Irvine, he was an upstate Yorker by adoption. I am one by assimilation. We both know the value of reticence. On that note, or near note, it is time to end this discussion. Do you agree?

Weren't you the first to interview these critics, and what do you think about the growing amount of work done about them?

To conclude, yes, these interviews are the first of this group, in part because academic writers have been thought to be of little consequence. So the interviews contradict that received wisdom. Nonetheless, there are books and articles appearing about the Yale four. Others shall no doubt conduct other interviews.

Are you going to continue writing about this group?

Probably not, perhaps yes.

You took some care to introduce biographical questions during the questioning. Anything to say about yourself?

All right, and this is the last question and response! I suppose that I was first drawn to *literature* as a form of instinctive release from the *fact* of a rural one-room schoolhouse, frame, with exposed rafters, and a potbelly stove which was heated red hot during the winters. One of the third grade teachers used this as a torture for the refractory, making them sit a foot or so away for red and sweaty punishment. That frame room, an institution of learning with its outhouses, was the setting for literary escape, of reading for more than its own sake. The same process continues in disguised but deeply alien contemporary environs to literacy. So lecturing and reading on and of texts such as Browning's somehow echoes in that third grade room, a shack on 4 × 4 stilts, when I crouched in the back devouring a borrowed eighth grade reader with its version of *The Song of Roland.* Perhaps readers of literature will always in some sense be put next to the stove for a kind of punishment.

Finally, however, I see that poetry itself has little to do with such biographical matters. The notation of music has much the same problem as the notation of poetry. The reading of each is part learning and part instinct, and each practice has a heavy overlay of rational or pseudo-programmatic comment which defies the subject itself.